God Loves You Circle

Short Stories
of
Christian Living

Michelle Johnson

GOD LOVES YOU CIRCLE

©2013, Michelle Johnson and Healthy Life Press
All Rights Reserved

Published by:

Healthy Life Press • 2603 Drake Drive • Orlando, FL 32810
www.healthylifepress.com

Cover and Internal Design: Judy Johnson

Printed in the United States of America

This book is protected by US copyright laws. It may not be transmitted to others via electronic file or printed copy. Ebook purchasers do have permission to print one copy for your own personal use.

Library of Congress Cataloging-in-Publication Data

Johnson, Michelle
   God Loves You Circle

ISBN 978-1-939267-78-8
1. Christian Devotionals; 2. Short Stories of Christian Living

All biblical references are from the King James Version of the Bible.

Most Healthy Life Press resources are available worldwide through bookstores and online outlets, depending on their format. This book exists in full color. Contact: healthylifepress@aol.com or visit: www.healthylifepress.com. This book also exists in a downloadable and printable PDF format, with color, from www.healthylifepress.com. Direct contact: DBBV1@ AOL.COM. Commercial eReader versions available at: www.eChristian.com; www.amazon.com, and bn.com. Redistribution of printed or eBook formatted copies violates international copyright law, and is strictly forbidden. Your honesty is appreciated.

God Loves You Circle

Short Stories of Christian Living

Michelle Johnson

Withhold not good from them to whom it is due, when it is in the power of thine hand to do it. Say not unto thy neighbour, Go, and come again, and to morrow I will give; when thou hast it by thee.

Proverbs 3:27-28

She perceiveth that her merchandise is good: her candle goeth not out by night. She layeth her hands to the spindle, and her hands hold the distaff. She stretcheth out her hand to the poor; yea, she reacheth forth her hands to the needy.

Proverbs 31:18-20

She openeth her mouth with wisdom; and in her tongue is the law of kindness. She looketh well to the ways of her household, and eateth not the bread of idleness. Her children arise up, and call her blessed; her husband also, and he praiseth her.

Proverbs 31:26-28

Thank you . . .

A very special thank you to all of my wonderful, supportive friends and loved ones who helped in the proofing of this book. Thank you, Judy, Liz, and Paige, especially. Thank you to all who encouraged me, and took the time to read and comment on my writings.

Thank you, most of all, to my loving husband and two amazing daughters, Samantha and Amanda. You are all the greatest gift a woman could possibly receive . . . thank you for your endless support and love during the writing of this book. I love you so . . .

Contents

Prologue

Chapter 1:
   Thank You, Mommy, for Loving Me More . . .   16

Chapter 2: A Little Pot of Oil   26

Chapter 3: Poor Eli   38

Chapter 4: Dealing With Nastiness   46

Chapter 5: Our Little Sparrow   52

Chapter 6:
   How Many Times Do I Have to Tell You?   58

Chapter 7: Putting the Girls to Work   64

Chapter 8: Temptations and Victory   72

Chapter 9: Elver Park   84

Chapter 10: Bless Those That Curse You . . .   92

Chapter 11: Set Your Affections on Things Above   135

Chapter 12: Biting the Hand That Saves You   108

Chapter 13: Pookie, Tucker, and Hampton   114

Chapter 14: Elijah, the Widow, and Giving   126

Chapter 15: Consider the Lily   134

Chapter 16: God Loves You Circle   142

Healthy Life Press Resources   148

Prologue

I know what it's like to be a sinner, and I know what it's like to have a Savior. I know agony and I know peace. I know defeat, and I know the blessed release of victory. I am not perfect. I sure don't know everything. But, what I do know is this:

I am, simply, a sinner saved by grace . . .

The earliest memory I have of my life is between the ages of four and six, and it is a terrible one. Having been lured into a secluded place, I was sexually assaulted. My childhood innocence would be repeatedly shattered by various men throughout my life. Additional incestuous encounters by an old uncle left me broken and confused.

I grew up as an angry, bitter child who learned to enjoy the attention she got as a victim. I looked for negativity in every situation, in every sentence, and reveled in the offences I could find there. I, literally, looked for something to set me off, and then I enjoyed running to cry about it.

My father and I never connected. A string of hurts from my end and his left a great divide between us. Our relationship was fragile, cold, and distant. Although we both said "I forgive you," he would die before we ever shared the love a father and daughter crave. He was a man to be admired for many reasons, but it would be too late for us when I finally recognized it. Our relationship had been terminally damaged.

> "Being justified by faith, we have peace with God through our Lord Jesus Christ . . ."
> (Romans 5:1)

Prologue

By the tender age of nine, I had attempted suicide. By thirteen, I was institutionalized for a suicide attempt, and by fifteen I was a direct-admit for a third attempt. I struggled with anorexia and, shortly, with bulimia.

I hated life, and I was pretty sure it hated me back.

I remained that way until the blessed day I met my husband, Rob.

I was twenty when this handsome young infantry officer entered my life. I didn't think much of him at first. He was nice, sure, but I was waiting for the "real guy" to show up and, along with him, the inevitable hurt. But, he never came. . . .

This guy stayed nice.

Rob has an attitude I have never encountered before. He is always happy. He sees the glass half-full, and can find the silver lining to every cloud. He lives life with a sense of levity, even in the face of trials and tribulations. When a person is accused of doing something wrong, he assumes they were "just trying to do the right thing," and sets about finding the truth without judgment.

He told me I didn't have to be enslaved to my past, I could be who I wanted to be.

And, so, I began to reinvent myself.

Still, the victim in me would rise up on occasion, and it wasn't until I received the Lord Jesus Christ as my personal Savior that my life would be eternally altered for good.

When the child in me would rise up, threatening to remind me of my past, the Lord responded:

> "By whom also we have access by faith into this grace wherein we stand, and rejoice in hope of the glory of God."
> (Romans 5:2)

> "When I was a child, I spake as a child, I understood as a child, I thought as a child: but when I became a man, I put away childish things" (1 Corinthians 13:11).

When I wanted to feel victimized and sorry for myself, the Lord said:

> "And he said unto me, 'My grace is sufficient for thee: for my strength is made perfect in weakness.'"

And I was able to respond: "Most gladly therefore will I rather glory in my infirmities, that the power of Christ may rest upon me. Therefore I take pleasure in infirmities, in reproaches, in necessities, in persecutions, in distresses for Christ's sake: for when I am weak, then am I strong."

As a saved adult, I encountered a new set of problems. The migraines I had been diagnosed with as a child became incessant and relentless. After a flurry of appointments, I found myself locked into a regimen of medications that would lead to years of dysfunction.

The combination trips to the ER every few days and my prescribed medical regimen threw me into hallucinations and near madness. I hallucinated twenty four hours per day, with my eyes open and closed, and had a difficult time discerning reality. I don't know how my husband handled it those two years. . . .

Eventually, he approached the doctors to start weaning me off the medications. I still had my headaches, and from Rob's point of view . . . if I

"And not only so, but we glory in tribulations also: knowing that tribulation worketh patience . . ."

(Romans 5:3)

Prologue

was going to suffer headaches either way, he would rather have his wife back in reality.

By the grace of God, and because of my good husband's hard work, our sweet daughters were protected from most of it. I was able to speak with normality when they were around, and so, aside from spending a lot of time in the hospital . . . they were generally unaware of the depth of the problem. Meanwhile, I saw things I don't care to ever describe to anyone. . . .

Through it all, the scriptures and the love of my family sustained me. But, the one thing that could always break the madness was the pure milk of the word of God. Rob would read to me daily to calm my fears.

As the medications were reduced, the clarity of my mind returned, and the hallucinations faded.

Since the moment I received Jesus as my Lord and Savior, I have had a passion for introducing people to Christ and helping them grow in their faith. I yearned for others to experience the same release from the awful strongholds that can become our defining factors. I prayed others could break the shackles that bound them, and learn to be free . . .

> "If the Son therefore shall make you free, ye shall be free indeed" (John 8:36).

The Lord has shown me that my life, from the very start, was meant to become my "platform" for ministry. He opened my eyes to the truth that, if I had not gone through any of it, my ministry could not touch the depths of the soul

> "And patience, experience; and experience, hope . . ."
> (Romans 5:4)

> "And hope maketh not ashamed; because the love of God is shed abroad in our hearts by the Holy Ghost which is given unto us."
> (Romans 5:5)

to reach another.

So, rather do I truly glory in my infirmities . . . because I have been weak I am now, through Christ, made strong.

And thus began my ministry with the Lord Jesus Christ.

My heart is to reach the world; to save the lost, heal the broken-hearted, release the captives, and restore sight to the spiritually blind.

"The Spirit of the Lord GOD is upon me; because the LORD hath anointed me to preach good tidings unto the meek; he hath sent me to bind up the broken-hearted, to proclaim liberty to the captives, and the opening of the prison to them that are bound; To proclaim the acceptable year of the LORD, and the day of vengeance of our God; to comfort all that mourn" (Isaiah 61:1-2).

Welcome to my story.

Chapter 1

Thank You, Mommy, for Loving Me More . . .

One evening, I was given a tremendous opportunity to demonstrate God's love to our oldest daughter, Samantha (six years old at the time). It was one of those rare and perfect lessons wherein the teacher became the student, and the student unwittingly became the teacher. I learned as much as she did on this very precious night.

All children are emotionally tender when they are ill; our two sweet girls are no different. Our family had been down for four days with stomach flus, and we were all tired and weak. At supper time this night, Samantha said her tummy wasn't feeling well again. Knowing both she and her sister, Amanda (3 years) had been touch-and-go for several days, we didn't push her to eat much.

My husband and I were running an online business, and I knew had a deluge of e-mails to sort through and answer. After dinner, I sighed deeply and, with my own tender tummy, I plodded upstairs to get to work. *A little quiet time on the e-mail might not be such a bad thing*, I thought. A few minutes later, I was deeply engrossed in answering e-mails.

While I was tippity-tapping away, I heard Samantha start crying downstairs. She wasn't just crying a little; she sounded completely distraught. I assumed she was just sick to her tummy, and I settled down as I heard the gentle sounds of my good husband, Rob, consoling her. I knew he would take good care of her, as he always does, and returned to my e-mails.

About five minutes later, Samantha walked into our bedroom emotionally broken. She was

> "Lo, children are an heritage of the LORD: and the fruit of the womb is his reward."
>
> (Psalms 127:3)

carefully carrying a picture I had sketched a few days earlier, and crying so intensely that she couldn't breathe or manage to speak a single word. This wasn't a screaming-fit, mind you, but rather soul-wrenching, heart-broken, heaving sobs. I have only seen her upset like that once in her whole life, and it moved me deeply.

Immediately, she had my full attention. I called her onto the bed, and she climbed up slowly, sobbing, with hot tears streaming down her face. Gently, she climbed right onto my lap, where she curled into the fetal position and continued crying. With tiny little shaky hands, she held out the sketch I had made. Hardly able to breathe, she pointed to a spot on the picture and, with tremendous effort, said, "I (SUP) . . . IIIIII (SUP) . . . got (Sup, SUP, cough!) . . . nooooodles! (Wail!)"

Slowly, I was able to put it all together. My poor, sweet, daughter's world had come crashing down around her . . . all because she had dropped a single noodle, with spaghetti sauce on it, on my picture. *Oh, baby*, I thought...and my heart completely broke for her. My darling Samantha was in anguish over a noodle . . . and the tiny little spot it had left on a picture I had drawn.

I drew her in close and wrapped my arms lovingly around her. "My darling Samantha," I said in warm, gentle tones, "don't you know that I love you more than a picture?"

Still coughing and sputtering, she nodded slowly, and said, "But, (sup), but (cough), you worked so *haaaard* on it! (cough, cough) *I saw you!*"

> "We love him, because he first loved us."
> (1 John 4:19)

Both of our girls are always in awe of what I draw. Now, I'm not a terribly good artist, but I have some natural artistic abilities. To them, though . . . there couldn't be an artist better than Mommy.

Samantha had watched me pull my subjects, and create a rough sketch from the book of Esther. In it, Queen Esther was before King Ahasuerus at his throne. She was on her knees reaching out to touch the scepter he had so graciously extended to her, an act of love which ultimately saved her life, and the lives of her people. It really hadn't taken me all that long to sketch—an hour or two tops. To a six-year-old, however, who truly understands the importance of doing your best and working diligently...it had been a *huge* project. Additionally, when she and Amanda had eaten near the picture a few days ago, I had asked them, gently, to be careful around it. It was only a first-draft, however, and I hadn't been too concerned with it.

Still, Samantha was crushed.

"Oh, honey," I said, "let's pretend that I loved this picture very, very much. If the Lord allowed it to get destroyed...what does that mean?"

(cough, cough, sup . . .)

"Well, darling, that simply means that I have a much better drawing than this one to make yet, and I should only be thankful that this one got messy. And I *am*, so *thank you*! Remember that God said that all things work together for good to them that love Him and are the called according to His purpose? Your mommy loves God very much, and I *am* the called according to His purpose. So, my love, this could only

"Whatsoever thy hand findeth to do, do it with thy might."
(Ecclesiastes 9:10)

work together for my *good*. A picture could never be as important to me as you are, no matter how much work I put into it. You are a greater gift to me than all the paintings in all the world that have ever been or ever will be. Besides . . . it wasn't even *your fault* for dropping a noodle on it, was it?"

She was beginning to calm down now, and looked up at me with questioning, swollen, red eyes.

"Samantha, honey, if I care enough about something and I really don't want you to spill something on it . . . well, then it's *my* responsibility to make sure it is put in a place where you can't!"

Relief flooded her face. I could just see the burden lifted from her, and she immediately melted into me for hugs and cuddles, which lasted for several wonderful minutes. Once her little pot was filled, and her soul soothed, she bounded happily back down the stairs to Rob.

That was the last I knew about it until prayer time that night, when I was completely overwhelmed with the maturity in Samantha's six-year-old prayer:

> "Dear Lord,
> Thank you for this wonderful day you've given to us. Are you coming today, Lord? I am looking for you. Come into my heart, and thank you for forgiving my sins. Thank you for Mommy, and Daddy, and Amanda, who is so sweet and adorable and loves to play puppy. Lord, thank you that my mommy said she

> "And we know that all things work together for good to them that love God, to them who are the called according to his purpose."
> (Romans 8:28)

loves me more than her picture. In Jesus' name I pray, Amen."

We tucked the girls into bed with hugs and kisses, and went back to our bedroom.

Rob turned to me and told me the rest of the story. Samantha had come running downstairs after talking with me, declaring "Daddy! Daddy! Mommy loves me more than her picture! *She said so!*"

Now, I have to admit...there was a little part of me that was disappointed to hear that. Of course, I was happy that she was happy . . . but, my goodness . . . one of our favorite "family-ism's" is to say, "Do you know what? I love you!" It's a contest to see who can blurt out, "I love you!" first and win. In our family, if you have nothing to say at all, you simply say, "I love you." It's a phrase we utter to each other countless times every day. So, there was that little part of me that was a little bit sad that I actually had to *tell her* that I love her more than a picture.

She had even gone to Rob a second time, and, holding the picture . . . she looked at him with wide-eyed wonder. "Daddy! She didn't even *see* the spot!" My good husband smiled lovingly and said, "Well, Samantha . . . that's because she was looking at *you*."

That's when it hit me . . . my darling Samantha had just seen God, and so had I.

Our loving God created all things for us richly to enjoy. As children, we watch in wonder as the Lord creates His perfect pictures. Perhaps the perfect picture He created for you is the child in your home, your husband, your finan-

> "As far as the east is from the west, so far hath he removed our transgressions from us."
> (Psalms 103:12)

> "For all have sinned, and come short of the glory of God."
>
> (Romans 3:23)

cial security, your house, your mentor, or your deepest friendships. Some days you are aware of His efforts and you watch in awe and wonder as He works diligently sketching the perfect picture of your life. On those days, we soak up the whole of His world for us, and appreciate every last detail.

But then, one day . . . we drop a noodle on it.

Immediately, we allow our soul to grieve. After all, we know how hard He worked, and all the love He put into His work . . . we were there, we *saw it*. But, there we go . . . carelessly ruining it. He had even warned us to be careful around the picture in the past.

Perhaps He had warned us against things that would ruin our picture, like being unkind to our children, irritable toward our loved ones, a poor steward of our house or money, or foolish with the wisdom we've been given. In a split second of carelessness, we become tormented over the very gift He worked so hard to give us.

Immediately, we go to Him. Sorrowful and racked with guilt, we curl up in His mighty lap holding out the ruined picture of our life.

Deeply our Lord sighs . . .

Oh, how terribly it grieves Him! His heart is torn...but not for the picture . . . never for the picture, darling. He is filled with sorrow for *our* pain. He doesn't care about the spill, child, all He cares about is that we didn't *know* He loved us *more than the picture*. He only wishes that we knew He made it for us because He loves *us*, not because He loves the picture. The Lord grieves because it created pain in the very heart it was made to fill with joy. He simply hoped that we would have known, after hearing it countless times every day, that, "You know what? *I love you.*"

God knows that we love Him. He knows it hurts us when we don't do things exactly right. He just wants us to say we're sorry and move on. When Jesus died on the cross, He took *all* of our sins with Him. Every single one of them was covered right then and there, not just our past sins! How could He have died for any of our sins if not for all of them? We weren't even alive when He died for us . . . all of our sins were in the future from the beginning.

Next time we drop a noodle and mess up God's perfect picture, let Him hold us in His loving arms and say, "My darling child . . . don't you know I love you more than that picture?" We should thank Him for the chance to do it better next time. Say we're sorry, and get excited about the lessons we're about to learn, or the better picture we're about to get . . . and then *move on.* Sitting in self-pity is keeping the focus on ourselves, and all God wants is our focus on *Him.* When our focus is on Him, we'll discover with wide-eyed wonder, that He can't even see our spot. Then, we will finally see ourselves as God sees us, looking right past all of our faults, and realize just how completely His sacrifice has cleansed us.

> ". . . though your sins be as scarlet, they shall be as white as snow; though they be red like crimson, they shall be as wool" (Isaiah 1:18).

"I have loved thee with an everlasting love: therefore with lovingkindness have I drawn thee."
(Jeremiah 31:3)

With a heart overflowing in gratitude and disbelief, you will see that you are, truly, washed whiter than snow. That's when all of the Heavens will rejoice because you finally realized it, refused to let yourself grieve, apologized to Him, and then, simply said...

"Thank you, God, for loving me more. . . ."

> "Herein is love, not that we loved God, but that he loved us, and sent his Son to be the propitiation for our sins."
>
> (1 John 4:10)

Notes and Reflections

A One-Sentence Prayer

CHAPTER 2

A Little Pot of Oil

What do you do when you are completely overwhelmed and exhausted? How do you handle family tragedies, death, divorce, loneliness, and frustration? How can one person possibly bear the burdens you bear in your life?

You can't handle them. You can't bear the burdens. You can't do any of it. Neither can I.

I have been reading about the young widow and her little pot of oil found in 2 Kings. It is hardly a wisp of a story, and if you blink, you might miss it. A brief seven verses long, it can be read in the time it takes to pour a cup of coffee. Yet, in this brief little story, there are volumes of wisdom and hidden treasures to be found.

It is about 800 BC, and our little widow's husband has just died. As she and her family mourn the loss of a great man, debt collectors begin to surface. Paying little heed to her personal torment, one of them quickly calls in her husbands' debts—payment due immediately. If she cannot pay, her two precious sons will be sold as slaves.

With little money of her own, the widow knows she is facing the very real possibility of losing her children. Soon, the last of her meager resources are depleted, and she is desperately searching for a way to keep her children. She cannot bear the thought of losing them in addition to the tragic loss of her husband. How much more can a woman's heart take?

Like all the other women she knew, the male authorities in her life have always served as spiritual guides. The Lord repeatedly calls out men as spiritual heads in the Scriptures, and she had

> "Save me, O God; for the waters are come in unto my soul. I sink in deep mire, where there is no standing . . ."
>
> (Psalm 69:1-2)

been taught well to respect that. She is resolved to do what she has been taught to do and, naturally, she chooses the most powerful prophet around.

She seeks out the prophet Elisha. Her husband had been a godly man; he was a son of the prophets (a preacher in training), and was well known. As she goes to Elisha, she is wrestling with her circumstances before God. She simply cannot understand why the family of a godly servant would suffer such an exceedingly harsh and lamentable trial. The God her husband had proclaimed to serve was supposed to be a loving God. Where is this love He proclaimed to her day after day?

> *"Thy servant my husband is dead; and thou knowest that thy servant did fear the LORD: and the creditor is come to take unto him my two sons to be bondmen"* (2 Kings 4:1b).

Elisha is well aware of the dire circumstances that the widow is in, and immediately realizes he has a significant opportunity to help. His heart is broken for her and he wants to do everything he can. He knows he could become her hero, calling for a collection to help this poor woman keep her family. If that wasn't enough, he could open up the church's coffers and offer her a gift to satisfy the debts. He possesses that power, and he has the authority to execute upon it. In a simple word or two, he could fix everything . . . which is precisely why the widow had sought him out.

"I am come into deep waters, where the floods overflow me. I am weary of my crying: my throat is dried: mine eyes fail while I wait for my God."

(Psalms 69:2-3)

Elisha, however, loved God ... and when you love God, it is Him you want glorified, not yourself ... your eyes are simply focused elsewhere. Elisha would not choose self-glorification, no matter how his human heart felt for her. Instead, he simply asks the widow what she has in the house. *Surely, he is discerning my needs so that he might meet them*, she thinks. She replies that she has nothing at all save a little pot of oil.

Much to her surprise and dismay, instead of opening up the church coffers and offering monetary assistance, he gives her some very odd instructions. He tells her to borrow vessels from all of her neighbors, close herself and sons up in the house, and then pour out the oil from her small pot into the borrowed pots.

Disappointed and cynical, she thinks, "Well, now ... what good could that possibly do?" She had done everything properly; she followed the right channels...why was she being brushed off? Hadn't her husband's faithful service meant anything to these people? Hadn't it earned at least a little help, a *little* compassion?

It seems that Elisha, the one person with the power and authority to help her, had chosen to set her about some pointless chores. She suspects his instructions are only meant as a distraction to fill her time as she nears the inevitable loss of her two sons. First her husband ... and now, surely, her sons. ...

She leaves with nothing but the word of God.

But, as awful as it seems, this was precisely the place that she was meant to reach. She is at the lowest of lows, with the most barren of cupboards, and filled with hopeless despair. But, it

"My soul doth magnify the Lord."

(Luke 1:46)

> "O the depth of the riches both of the wisdom and knowledge of God! how unsearchable are his judgments, and his ways past finding out!"
>
> (Romans 11:33)

is here that she had been brought to, where she would have no other choice but to abandon all sense of reason and look to God. In desperation, she draws in a deep breath, closes her eyes, and steps out in an act of faith.

As her neighbors look on, she instructs her sons to begin collecting vessels. They can all hear the neighbors murmuring amongst themselves . . . whispering that the widow has completely lost her mind, how sad they are for the family, how thankful they are it hadn't happened to them. Some blame her, claiming that God only smites the disobedient, and turn away in judgmental scorn. Some, however, loan vessel after vessel to them out of pity. *Poor, poor woman . . . she has lost her mind; such a tragic story, they think.*

Our little widow is numb, now; just going through motions. She is resigned to defeat, as one is when watching a loved one in the final throes of death. Her face is pale and expressionless as she busies herself setting up a place to pour her oil. She only intends to "check the box" and complete the one last task she was given by an authority. At least this way, when Elisha inquires later, others can truthfully answer, *Yes, she did it, right before she cursed your God and died.*

She heaves a defeated sigh as she pours the first little bit of oil from her pot into another. It trickles out slowly. She knows how little there is left, and after the initial pour, she steadies herself for the few remaining drips to stop.

Drip-drip, drip, drip . . . drip . . . . drip . . . . drip . . . . drip . . . .

Her heart fails for sadness as the last drop falls, and her hands tremble as reality sinks in. She had doubted it would work, but still, she had allowed herself the tiniest glimmer of hope. Her eyes widen in fear and her breath quickens. She lingers with her now-empty pot hovering inches over a borrowed pot.

Her hands are shaking visibly, and she can't bring herself to meet the gaze of her doomed sons. If only she could will it to keep pouring.

.... drip ......

Huh. There was still one drop left, she muses.

.... drip ....

Must have had a little bit of oil caught somewhere. She sighs heavily.

.... drip ..... drip ....

This is torture . . . just stop dripping so I can be done with this! I'm not going to buy into your false hope!

drip . . . drip-drip, drip-drip-drip

Wha. . . .? There couldn't have been that much in there. Could there? No . . . be realistic! It's just a pocket of oil. There must be a defect in the inner cavity, and when my hand shook, the oil broke free of it.

drip-drip-drip-dripDripDripDrip driiiiip, driiiiiip. . . .

It can't be! Can it? Her brows furrow, eyes narrow, and head tilts to one side like a curious child examining a new-found creature. Her heart begins to beat as hope shines its first rays on her darkened heart.

Slowly, a thick, golden stream begins to flow.

Her eyes grow wild in disbelief as the first vessel fills.

> "Hope deferred maketh the heart sick: but when the desire cometh, it is a tree of life."
> (Proverbs 13:12)

> "But they that wait upon the LORD shall renew their strength; they shall mount up with wings as eagles; they shall run, and not be weary; and they shall walk, and not faint."
>
> (Isaiah 40:31)

"Boys! *Boys!!* Grab another pot! *Quickly!*" Moved by the intensity of their mother's reaction, but still quite unsure of what is happening, they respond quickly. Pot after pot is filled as the oil pours more readily. The young men soon realize that ten large pots have been filled by their one small vessel, and understanding dawns on them. Hope beams forth from all three faces.

"Quick, boys! Set up all the pots! Hurry…I don't want to right it and stop the pouring! Gather everything in the house that can hold an ounce of oil! Did you get *every* pot from the neighbors?"

Soon, every pot, every ladle, and every little cup is filled to the brim with beautiful, sweet oil. With no more vessels to fill, and oil dripping from her sons' tightly cupped hands, our widow finally must right her little pot to halt the flow.

Her heart is pounding in her chest, and her knees are weak as she turns slowly to find her boys dripping in oil, and surrounded by countless little pots filled to the very brim. She knows oil is a type of the Holy Spirit, and as she looks at her young sons covered with it, she hears a gentle whisper echo through her mind, "Covered, protected, surrounded, and safe."

"It's a miracle . . ." she whispers breathlessly, as her eyes lift to meet the gaze of her sons, "We are saved! Oh, *thank you*, Lord!" They stare at each other, take in the oil-soaked scene around them, and with a giddy sense of bewilderment and joy, they all begin to giggle with the sheer release true salvation brings.

In wide-eyed wonder and disbelief, their hearts fill with love for the God who cares for them so very deeply. He had turned a hopeless situation into the lesson and blessing of a lifetime. She knew she didn't deserve it. She had been bitter and cynical. She had personified "Oh, ye of little faith," and knew she had poured out the oil in 99 percent doubt and a scant 1 percent absurd possibility. Yet, she had just watched in amazement as her pittance of faith produced salvation for her whole family.

Upon hearing her grateful recount, Elisha instructs her to sell the oil she had poured to repay her debts, and afterward, to continue pouring oil and selling it. Not only had God provided in a time of desperate need and hopelessness for her, he would continue to meet her needs daily.

This time, she had little doubt of what God would do through her. She knew all she needed to do was pour out, in faith, and He would amply supply all her needs. God had, indeed, been sufficient for her, regardless of her own weaknesses, in the midst of all her doubt, and through unimaginable tribulation.

It was never a question of whether the widow had faith in the pouring of the oil that filled those pots; surely she did not. It was not even a question of her faith at all, but rather the object her faith was placed in.

You see, it is never the strength or quantity of faith that is important for a successful outcome, but the innate strength that lies in the object the faith is placed in.

You can doubt, and even fervently deny that the ice on a frozen-solid lake will hold you up, and yet, when you get tossed out onto that lake

> "Now faith is the substance of things hoped for, the evidence of things not seen."
> (Hebrews 11:1)

screaming in fear, the lake *will* hold you. It will not give way simply because you choose not to believe it will hold you. It is solid, by *nature*, and cannot change . . . it is *you* who are not.

Conversely, you may loudly proclaim great and unwavering faith in the thin ice of another lake. You may be so confident that you choose to walk directly out to the center in an attempt to prove how faithful you are. Sadly, all the faith in the world will not stop the ice in that lake from collapsing beneath you. It is doomed to fail because the object of your faith is unstable and undeserving.

The widow was thrown out onto a lake that was frozen straight to the core. Failure was never even an option . . . it was *impossible*. Still, she agonized. It was a fearful and terrible thing, it was thrust upon her, and she did not like it.

God allowed her to get thrown onto the ice initially when her husband died, but it was Elisha who kept her there. Strangely, his actions are the mark of a true friend. "Faithful are the wounds of a friend" (Prov. 27:6), and it surely wounded him to turn her away as he did. If he hadn't, she would never have learned that God was sufficient to meet every single one of her needs. It was not Elisha's job to become an amateur providence in her life, but to guide her into a personal relationship for herself. He realized his job was to make himself as unnecessary as possible in her life.

She was, literally, forced to have an independent relationship with God so that He could prove He is the thick ice in her life. He was absolutely sufficient to meet all of her needs,

> "A friend loveth at all times, and a brother is born for adversity."
> (Proverbs 17:17)

abundantly . . . whether she trusted Him or not.

I love the representation of the Holy Spirit (oil) in this story. The widow had to pour herself out completely before she could be filled up again. That is precisely how the Holy Spirit works in our lives. God will not fill up our little pots of oil until we have first poured them out. Completely. Entirely. Exhaustively.

Are you waiting for patience, energy, peace, love, friendship, time, and money? Stop waiting and start doing. The Lord continually says to *go* and *do*, walk and run. He promises to guide us *while* we are going, doing, walking, and running.

> *"Give, and it shall be given unto you; good measure, pressed down, and shaken together, and running over, shall men give into your bosom. For with the same measure that ye mete withal it shall be measured to you again"* (Luke 6:38).

For the same manner in which you gave, the Lord will bless it back to you. Give love to get love. Give forgiveness to get forgiveness. Give, give, give . . . give until it *hurts* . . . until you are so tired, so poured out, that you can no longer focus your eyes. Give until you ache with the blessings you've poured out through the day...to your husband, your children, your friends, family, neighbors, mailman, and every soul you've touched that day. Love the ones who hate you and despitefully use you. Smile genuinely when all you want to do is hide and rest.

Go fill up your neighbor's empty pots with whatever is left in you. When you feel like your

---

"Withhold not good from them to whom it is due, when it is in the power of thine hand to do it."

(Proverbs 3:27)

day couldn't get any worse, bake some cookies for the lonely lady down the street. When you are feeling lonely and unloved, show a friend how much you love them. When you feel unappreciated and overworked, work hard at creating a way to show someone they are appreciated.

It is when you, like the widow, have reached the lowest low that you will finally look up. It is then that you will know you can't do any of this alone. Then, will you finally abandon all reason as you know it and ask Jesus to come into your heart, cleanse you of your sins, and fill you with the Comforter: the Holy Spirit. At long last, you will realize that you are completely crazy; that you are doing things that make no sense at all. You will finally have lost your mind and abandoned it to Christ, that He might live His perfect will through you.

You and I cannot do anything good, righteous, or worthwhile. Only Christ can do those things through us, and He can pour out so much more than we have inside that it will defy all logic, science, and reason.

Are you ready to surrender your will to God today? Are you ready to fill your neighbors' pots?

As Dwight L. Moody once said, "The world has yet to see what God can do with and for and through and in and by the man who is fully and wholly consecrated to Him. I will try my utmost to be that man."

The world has never seen what God can do through a woman totally surrendered to God's will. I intend to be that woman today . . . will you?

> "Commit thy works unto the LORD, and thy thoughts shall be established."
> (Proverbs 16:3)

Notes and Reflections

A One-Sentence Prayer

CHAPTER 3

Poor Eli

Bills are due. Clothes are needed. The pantry is bare. Gas is expensive. Need, need, *need*!

Must work. Must clean. Must be here, must be there. Must, must, *must*!

This was my day yesterday. Then, just as the girls were busy making projects (and huge messes) in the kitchen, I looked over my shoulder and something caught my eye. Amidst all the strewn shoes and backpacks, I saw something . . . what was it?

Then realization dawned on me . . .

Oh no! Dog poop!

But, as I got closer to it, something just wasn't right. Slowly the pools and drops of bright, red blood and stringy mucus began to register in my mind. I couldn't believe what I was seeing, and my heart sank.

Eli!

Our sweet fifteen-inch tri-colored beagle dog, Eli, is the most darling in all the world. His gentle nature and soulful eyes just beg you to love him. He is absolutely the sweetest, calmest, most loving dog you can imagine and his runt-of-the-litter status shows through in his extreme submissiveness. Named after Amanda's favorite prophet, Elijah, our Eli has been with us since he was a pup. He is such a good boy, and he even rings a bell to go outside.

"Mom, is that blood?" my fourteen-year-old daughter, Samantha, asked with great concern.

"Yes, honey," I said calmly and gently, "we need to get Eli to the vet right now."

"But, Mom, this is the second time!" she replied, clearly worried.

> "In the world ye shall have tribulation: but be of good cheer; I have overcome the world."
> (John 16:33)

"I know, sweetheart, let's just get him into the car."

My mind was swirling with questions and concerns. *What could he have gotten into? What if he swallowed another sewing needle like he did as a puppy? Could he have been poisoned? Ugh, what is it going to cost? Oh, Lord . . . what are we going to do? I can't afford a vet bill today! Help us, Lord, You have to provide for Eli . . . he's our baby! What do I do?*

The Lord immediately calmed my fears. There was only one thing to do: take Eli in and the Lord would take care of the rest.

A few minutes of frenetic activity later, and Samantha, our friend, Alicia, and I had piled into the car with Eli and were on the way to the emergency veterinary clinic.

I had such a sudden onslaught of "cares" piled on top of me that it was difficult to focus on anything else. Instead of praying to God as I drove, I found myself trying to plan out how I was going to afford the visit, and mentally preparing myself for the loss of our dog.

It was a true struggle trying to keep my mind stayed on the Lord. But, isn't that just how it is?

I was truly worried about how Eli would fare, and immediately the Lord brought this scripture to my mind:

> "But seek ye first the kingdom of God, and his righteousness; and all these things shall be added unto you" (Matt. 6:33).

With all the wrong that was happening around me, there was one thing that was hap-

> "A righteous man regardeth the life of his beast."
> (Proverbs 12:10)

pening right: I was seeking the Lord.

Every minute of the day we fight the rising of the cares of the world, which threaten to choke the word of God in our lives. If the Christian life is supposed to be so joyful, why is it we are always stuck needing or wanting something?

The answer lies not in what we have, but in Who we have. It lies not in what we see, but how we see it. In short: are we seeking our own will, or do we earnestly ache for the desires of God's heart?

I earnestly ached for the righteousness of God to shine forth in this situation, and that could only be found in taking our sweet Eli to the vet. There was no other way . . . and as I was able to re-focus my mind, I considered that scripture heartily.

The Lord brought my attention to the word: shall. "Shall" is a blessed word of promise in the Bible. So, what are the "all things" that the scripture talks about promising to add to us?

The answer is: what we eat, what we drink, our clothes, and even our very life, as Jesus taught:

> Therefore I say unto you, Take no thought for your life, what ye shall eat, or what ye shall drink; nor yet for your body, what ye shall put on. Is not the life more than meat, and the body than raiment?
>
> Behold the fowls of the air: for they sow not, neither do they reap, nor gather into barns; yet your heavenly Father feedeth them. Are ye not much better than they?

"The cares of this world . . . choke the word."

(Mark 4:19)

> "(God) is able to do exceeding abundantly above all that we ask or think, according to the power that worketh in us."
> (Ephesians 3:20)

Which of you by taking thought can add one cubit unto his stature?

And why take ye thought for raiment? Consider the lilies of the field, how they grow; they toil not, neither do they spin:

And yet I say unto you, That even Solomon in all his glory was not arrayed like one of these.

Wherefore, if God so clothe the grass of the field, which today is, and tomorrow is cast into the oven, shall he not much more clothe you, O ye of little faith?

Therefore take no thought, saying, What shall we eat? Or, What shall we drink? Or, Wherewithal shall we be clothed?

(For after all these things do the Gentiles seek:) for your heavenly Father knoweth that ye have need of all these things.

But seek ye first the kingdom of God, and his righteousness; and all these things shall be added unto you.

Take therefore no thought for the morrow: for the morrow shall take thought for the things of itself. Sufficient unto the day is the evil thereof (Matt. 6:19-34).

What a beautiful image it is to consider the intricate way the Lord delicately painted the beauty in a single lily. Have you ever stopped to consider the exquisite elegance of this short-lived flower?

Yet, the Lord says . . . with all the time and care He put into creating that perfect bloom which appears for but a moment in time, how much more does He care for you?

How much more did He care for me?

Resting in the Lord, and His promise of provision, we arrived at the veterinary clinic. After speaking with the doctor, and electing every diagnostic procedure to ensure the health of our dog, I turned to my husband, Rob, who had met us there, with pleading eyes.

He smiled sweetly and, putting his hands on my shoulders, said, "Don't worry. I enabled a funds transfer several days ago, and it's showing up tomorrow. We're fine. . . ."

I inhaled deeply and exhaled with my eyes closed, a wave of gratitude and love washing over me for the provision of the Lord and my dear husband.

Smiling, I thought to myself, *I should have known....*

Don't let the cares of this world choke the word of God in your life. Don't let your schedule out-commit a place for your Lord. Don't let your doubts overwhelm your faith.

What are the cares of this world that are choking the word of God in your life? Are you desperately focusing on work so you can pay your bills? Or are you committing your finances to the Lord and, with a thankful heart, resting in Him to be your Great Provider? Are you more concerned about your health than with spend-

> "Consider the lilies how they grow: they toil not, they spin not; and yet I say unto you, that Solomon in all his glory was not arrayed like one of these."
>
> (Luke 12:27)

> "(He) comforteth us in all our tribulation, that we may be able to comfort them which are in any trouble, by the comfort wherewith we ourselves are comforted of God."
>
> (2 Corinthians 1:4)

ing time with your Great Physician? Are you allowing yourself to worry instead of curling up with the Comforter?

If your heart is right toward the Lord, and you are seeking His will above your own, then the Lord has truly said, "My child, take no thought for it. I will always provide for you at just the right time in just the right way. I promise you: *All these things shall be added unto you.*"

Oh, and Eli? Well, $500.00 later, he was officially diagnosed with a bad case of the trots.

Notes and Reflections

A One-Sentence Prayer

Chapter 4

Dealing With Nastiness

One day, when my husband and I were running an online business, I received an e-mail entitled "Unsubscribe." It was common enough for us to get e-mails from people who were ready to stop their subscriptions; they were usually simple and non-descript. I opened this note expecting it would be no different.

Instead, I got berated. The man who had written the e-mail accused us of spam using such vulgarity and crude name calling that I blushed from head to toe just reading it. No matter how loose my language may have been in my youth . . . this e-mail left me embarrassed at having read it at all.

Although flushed, I was surprised at how truly not offended I was by such a harsh note. As soon as I finished reading the e-mail, the Holy Spirit brought this scripture to my mind:

> "Great peace have they that love thy law, and nothing shall offend them" (Psalm 119:165).

Having been so quickly cautioned that nothing was to offend me, I was truly nonplussed by the letter.

I love that the Lord explicitly says "nothing" is to offend me. He didn't say "only *worthwhile* things shall offend you." He said *nothing*.

When *nothing* offends you, then you can hug the person who just crashed into your car and praise the Lord for introducing you. Maybe the hug was the reason you wrecked in the first place. . . .

> "Peace I leave with you, my peace I give unto you: not as the world giveth, give I unto you. Let not your heart be troubled."
>
> (John 14:27)

> "That ye may approve things that are excellent; that ye may be sincere and without offence till the day of Christ."
>
> (Philippians 1:10)

When nothing offends you, you can wave to the guy who just flipped you off for making a mistake driving. Maybe he flipped you off because he needed a prayer. *"Bless them that curse you"* (Luke 6:28).

When nothing offends you, you can discipline your children in love and not anger. *"Keep thy heart with all diligence; for out of it are the issues of life"* (Prov. 4:23).

When nothing offends you, you can turn away anger with a soft answer. *"A soft answer turneth away wrath: but grievous words stir up anger"* (Prov. 15:1).

I praise the Lord that He gave me the wisdom to do just that in this particular situation.

Just a few short years ago, I would have been deeply offended and taken the e-mail as a personal attack. Instead, I was able to empathize with this man who was at his wits' end with spammers.

Instead of sending a defensive reply back to this gentleman, I was able to reply with kindness. I gently explained to him our policies and asked that the Lord bless him through his frustration.

I was surprised to see a reply from him later. He sent me a very nice note and apologized for his profanity. As it turned out, he was working hard to build his home-based business and had become frustrated with volumes of e-mail which distracted him from his goal.

Instead of just being insulted and returning the insult, we had a great opportunity to establish a relationship with this person.

What a blessing!

But, the greatest blessing is in knowing that the Lord can provide us with the answer to every day-to-day issue that comes up. He is not an aloof, uncaring God. He's ever-present, all knowing, and wise beyond comprehension.

What a delight it is that our Lord God has given us practical ways to handle the simple stresses in our lives.

Even in the face of this challenge, the Lord's response was much better than anything the old me could ever have come up with.

Let nothing offend you this week; not your children, your job, people's nastiness, or even something as big as a car wreck.

When you allow the Lord to live through you in a situation, you will have a peace that passes understanding.

> *"And the peace of God, which passeth all understanding, shall keep your hearts and minds through Christ Jesus"* (Phil. 4:7).

Your peace won't be your peace (something you have to force), but His peace (something you have to allow) and will be a greater peace than you could ever imagine. You won't just be saying that you aren't offended . . . you won't *feel* the slightest bit of offense at all.

"Trust in the LORD with all thine heart; and lean not unto thine own understanding. In all thy ways acknowledge him, and he shall direct thy paths."

(Proverbs 3:5-6)

Notes and Reflections

A One-Sentence Prayer

CHAPTER 5

Our Little Sparrow

"Are not two sparrows sold for a farthing? And one of them shall not fall on the ground without your Father. But the very hairs of your head are all numbered. Fear ye not therefore, ye are of more value than many sparrows" (Matt. 10:29-31).

Yesterday, a sweet little bird fell from the sky. My darling daughters, Samantha and Amanda (fourteen and eleven, respectively, at the time), found her hopping about our garage. She wasn't flying well.

Immediately, my girls begged to help her. They promised they would feed her, love her, and take perfect care of her.

"Find a box, and put her in it," I replied, smiling gently. I thought warmly of the countless pleas my own mother heard from me as a young child. *This will be good for them*, I thought.

The girls came in about ten minutes later, gingerly carrying a box with a makeshift lid. In hushed tones they whispered, "We got her! She's inside, but we don't want to startle her!" They slowly and delicately lowered the box and set it on the floor near my chair.

I pulled back the lid to find a strangely calm, mottled black and brown bird with a long beak. I reached in to the box and she allowed me to gently pet her chest and head. After a few minutes, she became startled and flew out of the box.

She couldn't seem to get altitude and only flew about two feet off of the ground. I was able

> "(The virtuous woman) stretcheth out her hand to the poor; yea, she reacheth forth her hands to the needy."
> (Proverbs 31:20)

to observe her well at this point, and came to the conclusion that she was simply a juvenile. She must have been out for her first flight when her underdeveloped wings failed her.

We recovered her, put her back in the box, and set about identifying her species. After a misidentifying her as a Yellow-Bellied Sap Sucker (to the great delight and onslaught of jokes from our whole family), we finally properly identified her as a Starling.

We researched her dietary needs, and were surprised to find that pulverized dog food was a mainstay in the diet of captive Starlings. It has the protein they need to support their system when they have an absence of their primary diet: insects.

It was bedtime by then, and Amanda, our youngest, immediately took the bird (now resting in a cat carrier complete with a perch, paper, water, and food) to her room.

"We decided her name should be Rachel," Amanda said. Then, she playfully added, "We also considered 'Snack' because of the kitties, but thought against it." We all laughed at their clever little joke, knowing that our two cats bring us wildlife nearly every day. "Snack" is what Rachel would have been had the kitties found her before our girls did. We were all thankful that our girls had found her first. . . .

As I lay in bed, Amanda came into the room, beaming. "Mom! Mom! You gotta come see! Samantha begged me to make you come see! Rachel's cooing!"

I opened the door to Samantha's room to find her sitting on a chair, lovingly petting the head

> "Study to shew thyself approved unto God, a workman that needeth not to be ashamed, rightly dividing the word of truth."
> (2 Timothy 2:15)

of a very sleepy and content little bird. Rachel opened her eyes to see me for a moment, and as I reached out to pet her head, she drifted back to sleep, gently cooing.

It was a priceless moment.

And I saw the Lord through the whole thing.
. . .

God has His eye on every little sparrow, and yet not one falls from the sky without the Father knowing. He knew this little Starling would fall yesterday and He orchestrated two of His favorite little saints finding her.

He cares so much for that little bird that He brought her to us, where she would be fed and cared for during the time she needs to grow. He brought her to a house filled with love and compassion because He cares for this sweet little bird.

If only we were able to see ourselves as the little Starling. . . .

During the time that we find our wings, sometimes we fail. God immediately sets in motion a plan that will provide for all of our bodily needs. He gingerly carries us in our little box of protection and leads us to safety.

We can choose to squawk and scream about it, but He's going to put us back in that box to protect us anyway. Sometimes, He reaches His hand into the cage and it startles us. We can choose to panic and flutter our wings, or we can choose to see He's giving us fresh water. We can choose to see terror and worry in everything, or we can choose to see love and provision.

When something frightens us, or threatens to make us worry, He has given us this Scripture:

> "What? know ye not that your body is the temple of the Holy Ghost which is in you, which ye have of God, and ye are not your own?"
>
> (1 Corinthians 6:19)

"And we know that all things work together for good to them that love God, to them who are the called according to His purpose" (Rom 8:28).

But, we must choose to accept the rest.

We are like that bird in the cage, and sometimes it frightens us when God changes our bedding. It's hard to remember He's doing it to protect us, because He loves us. He's doing it for our greater good.

Every detail of our lives, both good and bad, make up the greater composite picture of a life that is meant to bring great glory to God.

Allow God to change your bedding and freshen your water. As scary as it is, it is meant for your good.

Then curl up in His lap and fall asleep as He lovingly pets your head. He loves you to absolute distraction, dear one. . . .

We love our little "sparrow." Yet, greater are we to the Lord in Heaven who fashioned us with His own two hands; His love and care for us is immeasurable.

His love for *you* is unfathomable. . . .

> "For we which have believed do enter into rest."
> (Hebrews 4:3)

Notes and Reflections

A One-Sentence Prayer

CHAPTER 6

How Many Times do I Have to Tell You?

Today, I went upstairs with a happy heart to wake my daughters. I had let them sleep in until noon as a summertime treat.

When I opened the doors to my eleven-year-old daughter's room, I was shocked. Only a couple of short weeks ago, we had made sure that her room was nicely cleaned. Today, it looked like a hoarder lived there. She was sleeping on a bare mattress, and every inch of her floor was covered.

In order for her to walk anywhere in her room, she had to step on things. And somehow, at some level, she was actually okay with that.

How many times had I told her to clean her room that week?

How many times do I remind her to pick up after herself?

I was shocked and saddened, and I couldn't help but wonder how she could live like that when we have never raised her to live that way. Then fear hit me: if this is how she was going to live in our house, would she become that roommate that no one wants because of their filth?

Even with my heavy heart, I couldn't help but see the Lord in all of it.

How many times has He corrected me on behaviors I have?

How many times has He told me to pick up after myself?

Just as my daughter made my heart heavy today, I wonder how often I have made the Lord's heart heavy? How many times has He hoped I wouldn't grow up to demonstrate negative behaviors in ways that affect others around me?

> "Where no oxen are, the crib is clean: but much increase is by the strength of the ox."
> (Proverbs 14:4)

After all, He taught me perfectly. He taught me patiently. He taught me lovingly.

Yet, when He opens the door to my bedroom . . . what does He see?

As we set about chastening our daughter today, I am reminded of the Scriptures that speak of chastening.

> "He that spareth his rod hateth his son: but he that loveth him chasteneth him betimes" (Prov. 13:24).

> "For whom the Lord loveth he chasteneth . . . " (Heb. 12:6).

I love my daughter, and I will chasten her because I love her. Her actions need to produce an unwelcome result. She will lose her beloved computer for a time, for sure, and we will have to modify her behaviors. I don't want her to grow up accepting them. . . .

Today, I am thankful for the scripture:

> "Be ye angry, and sin not: let not the sun go down upon your wrath" (Eph. 4:26).

I am thankful for the Lord's reminder that it's okay to be angry, but punishing in anger is not okay. I am thankful for His peace that passes all understanding, which I can release into this situation to maintain His righteousness.

Because He has forgiven me exhaustively, I can easily forgive a messy room.

Because He has said about me: How many times do I have to tell you? I can say to her: I

"The LORD is merciful and gracious, slow to anger, and plenteous in mercy."

(Psalms 103:8)

understand, *and I forgive you.*

> "If we confess our sins, he is faithful and just to forgive us our sins, and to cleanse us from all unrighteousness" (1 John 1:9).

Dear Christian, He knows, He understands . . . *and He forgives you.*

> "Then came Peter to him, and said, Lord, how oft shall my brother sin against me, and I forgive him? till seven times? Jesus saith unto him, I say not unto thee, Until seven times: but, Until seventy times seven." (Matthew 18:21-22)

Notes and Reflections

A One-Sentence Prayer

CHAPTER 7

Putting the Girls to Work

While my children were very young (five and two), I hosted play-dates with a few other mothers. On this day in our history, my house was a mess to begin with, but by the time seven children and five moms had left, it was a disaster! Now, I was expecting a mess—because that's just what kids do—but seven kids under the age of seven can make an enormous, catastrophic mess.

In general, it doesn't bother me. This time, however, it stayed messy for four days. In my (meager) defense, my in-laws were out of town during those four days, and we were staying at their house to watch my young brothers-in-law (eleven and fourteen). The few hours we spent back at our place were used to work online, and other non-cleaning chores.

When we came home, I knew I had my work cut out for me. It would have been very easy for me to plug Samantha and Amanda into a movie, roll up my sleeves, and just "get it done." Instead, the Lord guided me to a better end.

After an uplifting conversation with a friend, I knew I wanted to see how the Lord would work through me in leading the girls to help.

Having committed this to Him, I knew exactly what I needed to do: It was important for Samantha and Amanda to understand responsibility and the work involved in cleaning up the messes they make.

> "Train up a child in the way he should go: and when he is old, he will not depart from it" (Prov. 22:6).

"Better is a neighbour that is near than a brother far off." (Proverbs 27:10)

If I cleaned up the mess myself, they would learn absolutely nothing, except that someone else will pick up their messes for them. No, thanks; that's not what I want my children to learn, and it's not the way the Lord would have us behave.

Every mother knows that teaching young children to help around the house often means the job will take twice as long, look half as good, and require double the patience on Mom's part. The kids may love to "help," but it can be hard for Mom to step back and not take over for the sake of productivity.

I had to die to my own desires to "just get it done" and allow the Lord to live through me for the sake of my children. He immediately gave me a plan.

I started by setting the timer on the oven. I gave the girls ten minutes to "beat the timer" and collect all of the toys that had migrated to their bedroom over the weekend. All they had to do was each fill a plastic bag and then dump it on our den floor (to be re-sorted and organized during the final clean-up). If they beat the timer, they got a gumball. If not, they continued on their chore.

Isn't that just the way the Lord works with us? When we are walking in His way, and in His word, He loves to reward us. Our God is a God of treasures and rewards, love and encouragement.

> "Prove me now herewith, saith the LORD of hosts, if I will not open you the windows of heaven, and pour you out a blessing,

"So then every one of us shall give account of himself to God."
(Romans 14:12)

that there shall not be room enough to receive it" (Mal. 3:10).

Thankfully, the girls beat the timer and were thrilled to receive their gumball, and a short break. I took the time to help them see their progress and praised them for the work they had done.

The Lord loves to commend us for a job well done. He corrects us because He loves us, and will praise us as we redirect our actions.

> *"For whom the LORD loveth he correcteth; even as a father the son in whom he delighteth"* (Prov. 3:12).

The next chore was more involved. It required cleaning the dining room, which was strewn with papers, pens, and toys. I set the timer again and they got straight to work. This time, they earned a chocolate-covered cherry and a small break before the next chore.

They did a wonderful job, and we moved on.

The final chore was to clean the bathroom with the reward being: one TV show and some carrot sticks.

The bathroom was the real challenge. Having the girls help pick up is completely different than scrubbing up lotion and soap messes. Picking up actually gets something done. Having children scrub something usually just means a bigger mess.

I gave our girls some non-toxic cleaning products, and showed them how to clean the counter and the mirror. As I expected, they

> "For precept must be upon precept, precept upon precept; line upon line, line upon line; here a little, and there a little."
>
> (Isaiah 28:10)

made considerably more of a mess than they cleaned up.

You know how it goes . . . they put down the clean paper towels to use a dirty sponge on the mirror. . . .

After they were done "cleaning" the bathroom, I praised and thanked them profusely. They beamed, and I set my pleased and accomplished-feeling little girls down to watch their movie. They had earned it.

Then, I went back, rolled up my sleeves, and scrubbed the whole bathroom again.

A little while later, the biblical truths that could be gleaned from our day struck me in a wonderful way. I saw my day with Samantha and Amanda in much the same way that I believe God sees His day with me.

Here I am: His child. Every day I bumble about my business, making mistakes as I go, and some days I just seem to let everything go to seed. At the end of the day, the good Lord brings me back to each of those areas of my life to clean them up.

Now, He *knows* it would be easier for Him to go "zap" and make those areas disappear from my life. Instead, for my own growth and edification, He chooses to instruct and guide me as I try to clean them up one at a time. I know I've done wrong, and am willing to work to clean up the messes . . . even though the job sometimes seems too big.

He starts me out on the easier projects so that I can see a real difference quickly, and then sends me a little blessing here and there to encourage me.

> "Whatsoever thy hand findeth to do, do it with thy might."
> (Ecclesiastes 9:10)

I take my gumballs and cordial cherries and give thanks. I relax a minute and then go straight back to find out what my next project is, thinking He must be the greatest Father in all the world.

In the same way that I lovingly watched and encouraged my girls, He watches me, beaming with pride, as I use the countertop cleaner on the mirror and smear it around with a dirty sponge.

I am just pleased as punch thinking that I am doing a great work for the Lord and that He is pleased that I am trying to please Him. All the while, the Lord is watching over my shoulder, encouraging and instructing me . . . *knowing* that He'll have a mess to clean up once I'm done.

Then, when I'm finished, He gives me a big hug and tells me how pleased He is with me.

So, I go off on my happy little way, thrilled that I let the Lord work through me and with me on a project. Meanwhile, God patiently mops up after me, making sure I don't slip and fall on the water I spilled on the floor.

I am not even aware that He's had to clean up after me, but someday, when I'm older, He'll pat me on the hand and chuckle as we recall this day together.

In the end, though, God *knows* that I learned something, that my heart was right, and that I did get some cleaning done. He knows that next time I will do better, and even better the time after. Eventually, as long as I continue to clean the bathroom with Him, He knows that I will get it right without even having to think about it. My instincts will become *His*. He will con-

> "Train up a child in the way he should go: and when he is old, he will not depart from it."
> (Proverbs 22:6)

tinue to patiently teach me how to clean the mirror properly, and, someday, I won't even think to do it any other way.

My very nature will be His . . . and my life will be completely hid in Him.

You can allow the Lord to work through you in any area of your life, and He will help you if you call on His name. We all need help. . . .

Some of us are struggling with the stress, patience, keeping our tongues, laziness, financial responsibilities, and so much more.

Thank God for the strength that is already in you, though Him, to deal with each situation. Make sure you commit each situation to Him before you go into it, and He will gently encourage you in the areas where you need help.

He won't expect you to get it right . . . He only wants you to approach that area through Him every time. Allow Him to live through you a little more each day, and someday. . . .

You won't even remember the time you used to clean the mirror with a dirty sponge in the first place.

> "Your life is hid with Christ in God."
> (Colossians 3:3)

Notes and Reflections

A One-Sentence Prayer

Chapter 8

Temptations and Victory

The Lord reminded me today that I cannot sit and wallow in self-pity and self-defeat. Rather, when I do the wrong thing, I confess it before Him, readjust my thinking (repent), and continue moving forward.

I was having a wonderful morning. I slept in until 8:30, then woke and exercised for thirty minutes. I spent some great time with the Lord in His word.

My youngest daughter was sleeping in a butterfly tent on my bedroom floor like a little angel. I had a cup of Starbucks Via. My husband had sweetly kissed me goodbye as he headed off to work, and my older daughter was at a sleepover, having a great time.

Life was grand, I was doing good things, and the Lord was living through me beautifully.

Then, I got a call from the dental office. I needed to go in and get some new impressions for my two daughters for orthopedic appliances. It sounds innocuous enough, but therein entered temptation. I'd previously worked at a dental office, so I knew how things ought to be. As a result, this phone call had the power to set me off to the point where I would end up saying things I shouldn't say. I complained, "Why didn't they get it right the first time? This is expensive, and it's such a hassle with two young children."

Admittedly, it felt good and right to vent. I'd feel great for the moment, victorious even, but then guilt would begin to nip at my heels. Within an hour, the perfect clarity of hindsight would settle in, and I would realize that during

> "If we confess our sins, he is faithful and just to forgive us our sins, and to cleanse us from all unrighteousness."
>
> (1 John 1:9)

> "For whom he did foreknow, he also did predestinate to be conformed to the image of his Son...."
>
> (Romans 8:29)

those "fleshy" moments I had denied the Lord's life through me entirely. I had lived entirely carnally, entirely of the flesh, and made comments based on feelings rather than facts. And how could I ever allow the Lord to live through me to help another while I was so focused on myself?

Ugh.

Haven't we all just snapped at one point or another?

Haven't we all said things we didn't want to, that we immediately regret, with words that were too edgy, in anger, or just plain wrong? Have you ever done that?

I sure have.

The Lord Jesus was perfect both in the flesh and as God. He *never* sinned. He *always* said the right things in the right way at the right time, exactly as would please His Father in Heaven.

The Lord's standard of living is always looming over me, and sometimes it can feel very weighty. You see, I want the glory of the Lord to shine through in every aspect of my life . . . as a wife, mother, friend, co-worker, church member . . . in *everything and all the time*.

All too often, though, I "forget God." All too often, I live in the flesh of the moment. I undo good things with doubtful disputations, I am imperfectly-tempered, forgetful, unkind, not tidy enough, too lazy, not thoughtful enough, and all-around *not perfect enough*. I didn't handle this right, I didn't do that right, I could've done this better. . . .

Every conversation, every e-mail, every action, every chore, every food decision, and the

Temptations and Victory

sum total of every day is always, ever being re-evaluated, scrutinized, and dissected for error.

It can be so exhausting, so humbling, and so completely discouraging. There is always another level to go to in my mind. There is always more I can do, better things I can say, more perfect ways to handle a situation. I can pick up the house, and realize it needs to be scrubbed. I can scrub the house and realize it needs to be reorganized.

Let's not forget nurturing and nourishing the kids, making money where I can, keeping the checkbook balanced, caring for my husband, caring for my friends, neighbors, family, pets, serving enough, reading my Bible enough . . . and the list goes on and on and on. There is, literally, *no end* to the things I should be doing in my mind.

And it just makes me think . . . *thank God I'm not God.* "Thank you, God, that Jesus lived the only perfect, sinless life that ever has been or ever will be . . . and *I can't recreate it!*"

I can't know the exact perfect answer to every situation. "For I know that in me (that is, in my flesh,) dwelleth no good thing: for to will is present with me; but how to perform that which is good I find not" (Rom. 7:18).

There is no controlling the flesh. It's simply not possible. We can only allow the Lord's Holy Spirit to live through us at any given moment of the day. We can't ever conquer the flesh, we can only allow the Lord to rise above it in and through us.

I prefer that people would look at me and think, "Wow, no one can do the things she does

> "Be not overcome of evil, but overcome evil with good."
> (Romans 12:21)

> "Though your sins be as scarlet, they shall be as white as snow; though they be red like crimson, they shall be as wool."
>
> (Isaiah 1:18)

lest God be with her." And, you know what? No one, anywhere, *can* do the things God prefers us to do lest God be with them.

When I first received Jesus Christ as my personal Savior, it changed me dramatically. Suddenly, the Bible made sense to me. And everything our pastor preached was like nectar from God Himself. It was delicious, and I couldn't get enough.

I truly understood grace, forgiveness, and the victorious Christian life at that time. I did the wrong thing constantly, but would just lift my head up to God and triumphantly thank Him for His grace and move on, guilt-free.

"Oh, well . . . *Grace!*" people would hear me cry out again and again.

I knew, and fully embodied the truth that the Lord's blood covered every ounce of my every sin, past, present, and future, and I claimed it relentlessly.

If there was anything I ever needed, coming from the life I had led, it was perfect grace from a perfect God, with boundless love, in a sinless, eternal form.

I knew from whence I had been saved. I understood the fires of hell I had been delivered from. I delighted in the laws Jesus came to proclaim: the laws of love, life, and perfect grace.

After a while, though, as happens in the lives of most Christians . . . I became aware of my sins as perceived by the world. Bit by bit, the Lord reshaped me and I began to put on the outward adornment of the Christian life.

Now, change for the better is good, mind you, and my changes have been very good. I know I need (and want) to be the kind of person that demonstrates, by grace, the godly characteristics that make others wonder what it is that I have that they are missing, including the fruit of the Spirit, as described in Galatians 5:22-23: "But the fruit of the Spirit is love, joy, peace, long-suffering, gentleness, goodness, faith, meekness, temperance: against such there is no law."

Sometimes people seem to view the fact that they have been saved by grace, through faith, as a license to continue in sin. They adopt the perspective that, "Hey, it's all covered . . . so, why not just play?"

Yes, Jesus came to die for all of our sins. Yes, there is nothing that we can do to separate ourselves from the love of God in Christ Jesus. No, that isn't a license to sin. The apostle Paul addressed this in Romans 6, which begins with, "What shall we say then? Shall we continue in sin, that grace may abound? God forbid!" If we have been made alive by grace through faith in Christ, the only reasonable response is to honor the life-giver by the way we live that life.

To put this into human terms, if you bought a car for your child, what would you expect? You would have truly worked hard and sacrificed to make such an extravagant purchase for them. A car is a big deal! Of course, your child would be ecstatic at receiving such a gift. But . . . what kind of behavior should you expect from them?

Some kids would be ultra-cautious, thankful, and respectful. Those parents would feel good about the gift and the way their child was using it. This is a child who honors their parents and

> "Likewise reckon ye also yourselves to be dead indeed unto sin, but alive unto God through Jesus Christ our Lord."
>
> (Romans 6:11)

> "Moreover it is required in stewards, that a man be found faithful."
> (1 Corinthians 4:2)

brings them joy. Those parents are going to be inclined to give their children more for having been so responsible and having made such good choices. As faithful stewards, they will be well-rewarded. This is a healthy relationship, and we recognize that easily.

What about the child who takes the car with momentary gratitude and immediately starts spinning out, picks up their friends, speeds, and even wrecks the car with friends in it?

Those parents are going to regret having ever given the gift. They will be ashamed and embarrassed of the whole situation. Their child will have caused shame, anxiety, and sadness. Their parents will continue to give to their child, because they love them, but they will give their child less in the future since they have been unfaithful stewards.

The Lord Jesus didn't come to die for us just so we could "take grace out for a test-drive" and run head-long into sin. We are expected to be responsible with the incredible gift we have been given.

If you had been the one to suffer and die as Jesus did —or better yet, *your child*, how would you hope people would treat that gift? If you had been the one to spend three days in hell, or better yet, *your child*, how would you hope people would treat that gift?

What if you, everyone you love, and the entire world was dying from a fatal disease—a horrible suffering death—and the one you love most deeply was discovered to have the cure in their blood alone?

What if, in order to save the world, the doctors had to harvest your beloved's blood and reproduce it? What if it was so urgent, and the need so vast that the only way was for your beloved to die in the giving of their blood? How deeply proud, and deeply saddened, would you be when your beloved decided to sacrifice their life for the salvation of all?

I can't imagine how proud I would be of my beloved turned a hero. I can't imagine how sad I would be for the deep sense of personal loss.

Still, I know I would really struggle if my child was the one to die, and I stayed alive to watch the results. At first, there would be sincere and deep gratitude for my beloved's gift. Some, however, would take it because they feel they deserve it. I would be sad for that, but keep my mind on those who had been grateful. In the moment, it would be a perfectly glorious thing.

But, soon, the glory would begin to fade. As the days, weeks, and years go on, only a few would continue to celebrate the life that was given for theirs and remember it throughout their day. Most would start to settle back into their lives with all of their healthy loved ones, and begin to let forgetfulness set in.

Some, who received the gift would turn around and use their health for horrible things. They would choose to continue in a life of abuse and cause damage to other people . . . other people my beloved had died to save.

I would be horrified to see men and women taking of the gift of life my beloved gave just to go out and destroy others. All that sacrifice just for a license to go back and sin? *Yuck* . . . and, oh, how I would struggle with hatred toward

> "What then? shall we sin, because we are not under the law, but under grace? God forbid."
>
> (Romans 6:15)

> "I am crucified with Christ: nevertheless I live; yet not I, but Christ liveth in me: and the life which I now live in the flesh I live by the faith of the Son of God, who loved me, and gave himself for me."
> (Galatians 2:20)

those people, but I would choose to focus on those who were grateful, and try to stay positive.

I would be so sad, and so ashamed as the years go by that my beloved's heroic gift had gone for the propitiation of sin and abuse instead of love, health, and gratitude. Wouldn't you? Don't you think the Father Who sent His Son to die for us expects more from us?

He does. He absolutely does. He rewards His faithful stewards. He rewards those who treasure the gift of sacrifice His Son gave for us. He rewards those who continue to *love Him* in their day to day walk.

Can't you see why running headlong into sin and claiming grace is foolish and unreasonable? When you accept Jesus Christ as your Savior, your life should be deeply changed.

He died for my sins, and for my eternal place in Heaven . . . and I want my life to reflect the gratitude I have for that gift. And I want my life to express forgiveness, following the apostle Paul's advice:

> "And be ye kind one to another, tenderhearted, forgiving one another, even as God for Christ's sake hath forgiven you" (Eph.4:32).

I ran head-long into sin today. We can't be perfect, and things like that will happen. I am thankful that, because our Savior died for me I can confess that sin before Him, readjust, and go from "being sad to being awesome instead." I can put the sin behind me immediately and go forward to good and right things, claiming victory over the defeat.

Remove yourself from, or limit your exposure to, potentially damaging situations and enter into the joy of the Lord in righteousness. Keep your conversation kind, encouraging, and loving to one another . . . not because you *have* to, but because you truly, deeply respect the gift of eternal life given to you when our Lord rose from the grave. This is the fountain of water He described as follows:

> "*. . . whosoever drinketh of the water that I shall give him shall never thirst; but the water that I shall give him shall be in him a well of water springing up into everlasting life*" (John 4:14).

Please drink of His gift responsibly. . . .

> "Now our Lord Jesus Christ himself . . . hath given us everlasting consolation and good hope through grace, comfort your hearts, and stablish you in every good word and work."
> (2 Thessalonians 2:16-17)

Notes and Reflections

A One-Sentence Prayer

CHAPTER 9

Elver Park

All morning long, Amanda (ten years old) had been pressing us to go to Elver Park to sled. Elver Park has a beautiful, long sledding hill and is popular throughout the city of Madison, Wisconsin.

Rob and I were undecided most of the morning. The temperature was reading 5 degrees, and we simply weren't sure if it was wise to go sledding in such frigid weather.

As the morning progressed into the early afternoon, the temperatures rose steadily. By noon, it was closer to 20 degrees . . . perfect sledding temperature.

I did not feel much like sledding, having the urge to write this day. I needed to get an introduction written for my book, so I could get it finished by the end of the day. A shortage of boots and warm weather gear ensured I couldn't sled with everyone.

Still, I wanted to go with my family. I enjoy watching the girls and Rob have fun on the sledding hill, and I decided I could write from the warmth of the car while watching them play.

Getting ready to leave became quite the production. Samantha's snow pants were too short (and, more importantly *too pink* for our young teen), the car was a mess and needed to be cleaned out, my tires were so low on air that they were almost flat, and I was in dire need of a Starbuck's White Chocolate Peppermint Mocha.

While cleaning out the car, I found a new Bible I had recently been given. I set it in my lap with the pile of Sunday school books I had gathered. My plan was to write my introduction and get ahead in my Sunday school lessons for

> "Every wise woman buildeth her house . . ."
> (Proverbs 14:1)

> "And we know that all things work together for good ~~to them~~ ~~that love~~ God, to them who are the called according to his purpose."
>
> (Romans 8:28)

the next week.

Once everything was done, and the sleds were loaded, we began to formulate our route. . . .

First, to the gas station to fill my tires. Next, to Starbucks to make my tummy happy. Then, to Erewhon for snow pants, and finally to Elver Park.

The first gas station we stopped at had air, but the pump was out of order. Pressing on, we drove in to town headed for the next nearest gas station, a Mobile Station on Highway 14 in Middleton.

As we stopped at red light, Rob had his turn signal rhythmically signaling our intent to turn left into the station. We sat and watched the light, when suddenly . . .

THUD!

We just blew a tire! I thought. It wasn't long before reality sank in: *We just got hit by a car!*

"Girls, are you okay?" I asked, concerned.

"Yes, we're fine . . . what happened?" they replied, wide-eyed.

Instinctively, I picked up my phone to call the police, but something made me hesitate. Rob put out his hand and said gently "Just wait. . . ."

He stepped out of the car to inspect the damage. A man in his late fifties stepped out of his dark blue Toyota truck. He had a bright white beard and mustache, and was wearing a red knitted cap and red down coat.

"Let's see what we've got," Rob said calmly.

"I don't think it was anything, I think it just broke the ice on the bumper," replied the gentleman.

"You're right, there doesn't seem to be any

damage. So, let's call it a, literal, "ice breaker!" *Hi, I'm Rob Johnson.*" He reached out his hand and shook the gentleman's heartily.

Rob got back into the car.

"Damage?" I asked.

"No, nothing," he replied. "It was an ice breaker."

He proceeded to tell me what had transpired between himself and the gentleman. We laughed, but just as the light turned green, I realized I had that new Bible in my lap.

"Oh," I said, "I should have given him this Bible!" I knew that he was turning the same direction that we were.

"Honey, if he pulls into the gas station, too, we should give him the Bible," I said.

"Okay," Rob replied.

We turned left into the gas station, and my heart sank as the gentleman drove on past. Rob pulled up to the air station, thankful to finally be there.

I looked up to see the dark blue Toyota pull into the back entrance of the gas station. *It's him!* I thought.

Rob had already met the man, so I asked him to give the Bible to him.

"Why don't you do it?" he asked encouragingly.

"Okay," I replied.

Amanda blurted out, "Mom! Can I go with you?"

I smiled, "Sure, honey."

Amanda and I got out of the car, and walked over to the truck as it filled with gas. The gentleman saw us coming and walked toward us,

"A merry heart doeth good like a medicine."
(Proverbs 17:22)

smiling.

"I hope I didn't scare you too much," he said timidly.

I smiled big and kept walking toward him, reaching out, I shook his hand. Amanda reached out and shook his hand, and with a smile said, "Hi, I'm Amanda."

I smiled, proud of my girl, "You know, I just finished writing a book, and one of the sections talks specifically about not being offended even if you get hit by a car. The scripture is . . . hmmm . . . *peace? Nothing shall . . .*" my mind went blank, and I looked off to the side for a second with my brow furrowed. "Oh! *Great peace have they that love thy law, and nothing shall offend them!* Hi, I'm Michelle."

"I'm Ron." He replied.

"This is for you, my dear," I said holding out the King James Bible to him.

"Thanks!" he said earnestly, smiling.

"You're welcome!" I smiled, and Amanda and I turned and walked away. As we walked away we gave a little high-five to each other and smiled triumphantly.

Back in the car, I realized I hadn't given him any way to contact us to establish an ongoing relationship.

What if he has questions? What if we're supposed to lead him to the Lord, or invite him to church?

Quickly, I jotted down my Facebook name and our home phone number on a pastel pink sticky note.

"Amanda, honey, would you run this back to Mr. Ron and tell him Mommy and Daddy would

---

"And he said unto them, Go ye into all the world, and preach the gospel to every creature."

(Mark 16:15)

like to be friends on Facebook and to give him a copy of my book?"

"Sure, Mom!" Amanda bounded happily off to deliver the note and the message.

I popped open Facebook, and updated my status, hoping that my Christian friends would pray for Ron.

We went on to Elver Park, where we discovered we had left Rob's hat and gloves at home. He went down the hill once, Samantha went three times, and Amanda four. Rob's hands were burning from the cold, Samantha hurt her wrist, and Amanda banged her head.

It was a total flop.

Yet, I stand in awe of the Lord today. . . .

Outside of Christ, there are so many real reasons to be frustrated today. We couldn't get out of the house smoothly. The car was a mess. We had to purchase snow pants last minute. The first store didn't have any that worked. We got into an accident. Plus, after spending money on new snow pants, the sledding trip was a total bomb and everyone got hurt.

Jesus said:

> *"In the world ye shall have tribulation: but be of good cheer; I have overcome the world"* (John 16:33).

The apostle Paul wrote,

> *"We know that all things work together for good to them that love God, to them who are the called according to his purpose"* (Rom. 8:28).

> "For my thoughts are not your thoughts, neither are your ways my ways, saith the LORD."
>
> (Isaiah 55:8)

It's a promise. In the world we *shall* have tribulation. There was no small amount of potential tribulation for us today, but, here we are, driving home and we think we've had a *great* day. In Christ, we were able to *"be of good cheer"* because we know that this is all part of the *"all things"* working together for our good.

We were able to find joy because we had spent the day together, got new snow pants, didn't sustain damage in the accident, met a new friend, and had the chance to be a great testimony in front of the girls.

In Christ, we have the unique and treasured opportunity to live in the Kingdom of God. As we go about our day, we can rest knowing that the Lord has orchestrated every moment of our day for His perfect will.

We don't know what the end of the story is with Ron. Perhaps he'll friend us, perhaps one of his friends will hear his side of story of today and lead him to Christ. Perhaps he's the entire reason we went out today. . . .

> "The kingdom of God is within you."
> (Luke 17:21)

Notes and Reflections

A One-Sentence Prayer

CHAPTER 10

Bless Those That Curse You . . .

*R*ecently, I joined a website called Authonomy.com. It's a hub for authors to gather and share their work with each other. The draw for authors to join the site is that it's run by HarperCollins, a major traditional publisher. HarperCollins watches the books as they are rated by the community and pulls the top five for the editor's desk every month, a highly coveted position.

I joined the site for the same reason as everyone else: the hope that my books might be picked up by a traditional publisher.

On the site, there is a bulletin board . . .and on the bulletin board, there is a place to share "good news."

Last week, as I lay racked with fever for two days, I submitted my book proposal to publishers in hopes of securing a publishing contract. I have read countless stories from authors saying that the wait between a submission and an answer can be quite long, and not to expect an immediate "Yes!"

Still, from the moment I submitted the proposals to this very moment, I find myself leaping at every e-mail notification hoping for good news.

I was shocked and delighted when, after only forty-eight hours, I actually did receive my first offer of contract from a wonderful small Christian publisher. Wow!

Once I confirmed that the offer was legitimate and had a chance to review the contract, in my state of elation, I quickly went to Authonomy's "good news" bulletin thread to share the good news! After all, that's what the thread is

> "I wait for the LORD, my soul doth wait, and in his word do I hope."
> (Psalms 130:5)

there for, right?

I wrote my exuberant posting and waited expectantly for the wave of congratulations from fellow authors who truly shared in my delight.

What followed was quite the opposite . . . and quite the shock.

An onslaught of venomous hatred poured out of the screen back at me.

My cheeks were hot and flushed as I read accusation after accusation, and unkindness after unkindness. *What? What did I do to deserve this?*

They *hated me.* Not because I had done anything wrong, mind you, but for no other reason than the subject I choose to write about: the Lord Jesus Christ. They slandered my writing and slammed my books publicly.

Immediately the Lord reminded me that, even when He was falsely accused . . . He did not defend Himself. He stood silently and took the fiery darts. And I was reminded of His words, "If the world hate you, ye know that it hated me before it hated you" (John 15:18).

The comfort of the Holy Spirit washed over me as He gently spoke to me:

> *"Blessed are they which are persecuted for righteousness' sake: for theirs is the kingdom of heaven"* (Matt. 5:10).
>
> *"Bless them that curse you, and pray for them which despitefully use you"* (Luke 6:28)
>
> *"Bless them which persecute you: bless, and curse not"* Rom. 12:14).

> "Marvel not, my brethren, if the world hate you."
> (1 John 3:13)

As I thought on those Scriptures, love began to well up in my heart for the souls of the people who hated me. I imagined them in the lake of fire for eternity, and my heart broke for them. . . .

As they poured out filth and lies about me, all I could feel was deep sorrow because they were clearly demonstrating where they had chosen to stand: against the God who loves them so much He died for them.

Emboldened and softened by the scriptures, I began to formulate a plan. . . .

If the Lord loves them so much He willingly died for them . . . I would love them so much that He becomes life to them.

> "Let no man seek his own, but every man another's wealth" (1 Cor. 10:24).

I was no longer going to seek my own promotion and success on this site…I was going to seek the promotion and success of everyone else. Lord willing, it would be for the benefit of my attackers and would impact their life in a positive way.

So, I began a new thread: "*How* I got a contract in 48 hours. . . ."

My new thread is a daily update on my experience with publishing. I am being completely open and making every ounce of it available to everyone . . . even my own prized proposal. I will lead, guide, and direct everyone else into getting their own publishing contracts, and even if I never get published myself, I will know that I have poured out love with every ounce of me to everyone else.

"But I say unto you which hear, Love your enemies, do good to them which hate you."

(Luke 6:27)

> "Let no man seek his own, but every man another's wealth."
> (1 Corinthians 10:24)

I will not seek my own wealth, but the wealth of others.

I will seek their success above my own.

I will bless those that have cursed me, and let the Lord pour out a love they cannot understand, and cannot contain.

Where is the persecution coming from in your life? What evil onslaught has left you feeling off-balance and insecure? Bless those that curse you, dear one . . .

In the end, you will be the one blessed by it, but not because you seek the blessing; but because you have sought the Blessor.

Notes and Reflections

A One-Sentence Prayer

Chapter 11

Set Your Affections on Things Above

One of my friends recently made this comment: "I really need to stop getting my hopes up high because it's such a disappointment when it doesn't go the way I want it to."

Sometimes, it can be so hard to deal with the disappointments that life can bring. We get the perfect scenario set in our minds, and really feel let down when reality doesn't meet our expectations. I know I sure do.

We are promised that in this world, we will have tribulation. *"In the world ye shall have tribulation: but be of good cheer; I have overcome the world"* (John 16:33).

> *"Beloved, think it not strange concerning the fiery trial which is to try you, as though some strange thing happened unto you. . ."* (1 Pet. 4:12).

We are promised a trial that *will try us*, and we aren't supposed to be surprised when it comes. So, what do we do? How do we make it through the trials? And, more importantly, how do we have victory over them?

We must die to ourselves and let Christ live through us.

We have to *die* first, not physically but spiritually. We have to die to our own wants and desires and allow Christ to live *through* us.

The apostle Paul said:

> *"I am crucified with Christ: nevertheless I live; yet not I, but Christ liveth in me: and the life I now live in the flesh I live by the*

"Why art thou cast down, O my soul? and why art thou disquieted in me? hope thou in God: for I shall yet praise him for the help of his countenance."

(Psalms 42:5)

"I am crucified with Christ: nevertheless I live; yet not I, but Christ liveth in me: and the life which I now live in the flesh I live by the faith of the Son of God, who loved me, and gave himself for me." (Galatians 2:20)

faith of the Son of God, who loved me and gave himself for me" (Gal. 2:20).

He said he has died to the flesh in Christ, identified with the suffering on the cross, and now the life that he lives is not his own. He has presented his body a *living* sacrifice unto God that his body would be used as a vehicle for the Lord to move through.

"Present your bodies a living sacrifice, holy, acceptable unto God, which is your reasonable service" (Rom. 12:1).

The Lord needs a "vehicle" to work through on this earth. He has limited Himself to working through the body of a believer in present history. If you think of our bodies as cars, we have to vacate the driver's seat and allow the Lord Jesus to drive for us.

We have to *allow* Him to live through us. We have to let go of control, and *let Him drive*. It's scary, it's intimidating, but it's *His will*.

Jesus said, *"Verily, verily, I say unto you, Except a corn of wheat fall into the ground and die, it abideth alone: but if it die, it bringeth forth much fruit"* (John 12:24).

If we die to ourselves, *then* our lives can bring forth much fruit.

The Lord truly wants a victorious and joyful life for you. He is simply waiting to drive. He wants to *"open you up the windows of heaven, and pour you out a blessing, that there shall not be room enough to receive it"* (Mal. 3:10).

So, how do you release the blessings of God

in your life?

Sometimes, the Lord will re-orchestrate your life and situation. Sometimes, He will simply enable a perspective change on your part. Either way, the Lord only *ever* releases the blessings if you are *seeking Him first*.

> "Therefore I say unto you, Take no thought for your life, what ye shall eat, or what ye shall drink; nor yet for your body, what ye shall put on. Behold the fowls of the air: for they sow not, neither do they reap, nor gather into barns; yet your heavenly Father feedeth them. Are ye not much better than they?" (Matt. 6:25).

> "Seek ye first the kingdom of God, and his righteousness; and all these things shall be added unto you" (Matt. 6:33).

The Lord promises to release the physical blessings when you are first seeking the kingdom of God and His righteousness.

It's a paradigm shift . . . a matter of where our focus is.

When you seek the blessing and not the Blessor, you're missing the boat.

God says, *"Come unto me, all ye that labour and are heavy laden, and I will give you rest"* (Matt. 11:28).

> "Call unto me, and I will answer thee, and shew thee great and mighty things, which thou knowest not" (Jer. 33:3).

"Prove me now herewith, saith the LORD of hosts, if I will not open you the windows of heaven, and pour you out a blessing, that there shall not be room enough to receive it."

(Malachi 3:10)

> "And when Peter was come down out of the ship, he walked on the water, to go to Jesus."
>
> (Matthew 14:29)

The act is to *first* seek Him, to *first* come unto Him, *first* to call unto Him, as Peter did on the Sea of Galilee.

Jesus was not the only one to walk on water in the Bible. Peter also did.

In Matthew chapter 14, Jesus performed the miracle of feeding the five thousand men (plus their women and children). Afterward, He told his disciples to get into a ship and go to the other side of the Sea of Galilee. Then, Jesus sent the masses of people away, and went off to pray alone.

Meanwhile, the disciples in the ship were in the midst of the sea and a terrible storm.

Late in the evening, Jesus went to join them by walking on water.

The disciples were frightened at first, believing Jesus to be a spirit, but Jesus calmed them immediately by saying, "Be of good cheer; it is I; be not afraid."

Peter shows remarkable faith now, and calls out to Jesus "Lord, if it be thou, bid me come unto thee on the water."

And Jesus said, "*Come.*"

Peter climbed out of the boat, and, amazingly, he *walked on water* toward Jesus. After a few steps, however, he saw the wind as boisterous as it was, and became afraid. Immediately, he began to sink and cried out to Jesus saying "Lord, save me!"

Immediately, the Lord stretched forth his hand, caught Peter, and saved him. The Lord replied to Peter "O thou of little faith, wherefore didst thou doubt?"

But, as long as Peter had his eyes focused on

the Lord Jesus, he was *able to walk on water*. When he stepped out in faith, with his eyes locked on the Lord's, he was able to do miraculous and wondrous things.

As soon as Peter got distracted, as soon as his attention was pulled away from Jesus, as soon as he noticed the storm he was in the midst of . . . *he sank*.

We are all in a storm of some sort, but the Lord can only work miracles in our lives when our focus is on Him. We have to *seek Him first*. . . .

The remarkable part is that Peter was a *man*. Unlike Jesus, he was *not* God. There was nothing supernatural about him. He was just a regular person like you or me but, for a moment he kept his eyes so firmly on the Lord, and trusted in Him so perfectly, that he actually walked on water.

Wow. . . .

Through this experience he learned, and through him, we learn the importance of this exhortation:

> "Set your affection on things above, not on things on the earth" (Col. 3:2).

> "Delight thyself also in the LORD: and he shall give thee the desires of thine heart" (Ps. 37:4).

In this story, Peter "delighted" himself in the Lord. Now, that doesn't mean just to have giddy joy in the Lord, although that is certainly part of delighting. Delighting means to, literally, *delight* yourself; to take the light off of you and put

> "I have heard of thee by the hearing of the ear: but now mine eye seeth thee."
> (Job 42:5)

> "(God) is able to do exceeding abundantly above all that we ask or think, according to the power that worketh in us."
> (Ephesians 20:20)

it on the Lord Jesus. If we are in the spotlight, our attention is on ourselves. Put the spotlight on Jesus . . . *delight* thyself in the Lord and *then* he *shall* give you the desires of your heart.

Giving you the desires of your heart is a twofold promise. He will not only give you the things your heart actually desires (*"every good gift and every perfect gift is from above . . ."* James 1:17), but He will begin to orchestrate and create the new desires of your heart.

> *"Commit thy way unto the LORD; trust also in him; and he shall bring it to pass"* (Ps. 37:5).

> *"Trust in the LORD with all thine heart; and lean not unto thine own understanding. In all thy ways acknowledge him, and he shall direct thy paths"* (Prov. 3:5-6).

> *"Godliness with contentment is great gain"* (1 Tim. 6:6).

I love the order of that last Scripture:

1. Godliness = You're allowing the Lord to live through you.
2. Contentment = You will experience contentment because of it.
3. Great Gain = Your spiritual life will have great gain.

Keep your eyes on Him, with thanksgiving and contentment. Seek His will and His blessing in everything, and He will give you the desires of your heart. First, you have to *let Him* by keeping your eyes locked with His. . . .

Seek the *Blessor*, and you'll unlock the *blessing*. . . .

> Set your affection on things above, not on things on the earth."
> (Colossians 3:2)

Notes and Reflections

A One-Sentence Prayer

Chapter 12

Biting the Hand That Saves You

Yesterday, I came downstairs to the sound of frantic scurrying. I could hear claws tearing at the carpet as my cats chased after something. It wasn't long before I saw the little brown streak of a chunky chipmunk trying desperately to escape the feline claws of death.

Knowing I needed to intervene to save the little critter's life, I ran right to him. He scampered up the couch where I was able to catch him for a moment, but he clawed and twisted his way out of my hands. Dropping to the ground, he ran into the dining room. I caught him again, and again he frantically writhed his way out of my grip.

I sure hope he doesn't bite me; if only he could understand I'm trying to help!

This time he scurried up our grandfather clock, stopping on the lower ledge; just within my reach. My hand shot out, and I wrapped my fingers around the chipmunk's swollen belly. This time, no matter how much twisting he did, my grip was sure. I was not going to let this sweet little chipmunk die at the paws of my kitties.

He turned just the right way, squared his face with my left index finger and . . .

Crack! I could hear the sound of my skin popping and his sharp teeth bouncing off bone. *Ouch!*

I hastened to open up the back door and gently tossed him outside, quickly shutting the cats inside.

Immediately, I squeezed my finger to flush out the wound with blood, helping to prevent

> "A prudent man foreseeth the evil, and hideth himself."
> (Proverbs 22:3)

> "For God hath not given us the spirit of fear; but of power, and of love, and of a sound mind."
>
> (2 Timothy 1:7)

infection and rabies. After washing and disinfecting my finger, and doing a thorough Google search on whether I needed to seek medical intervention, I was satisfied that my risk of rabies was low enough to stay home.

After a few minutes, I settled into my favorite chair and reflected on what had just happened. That poor little creature was scared for his life, and rightfully so. If he had stopped running, my little hunter and huntress would have pounced right away. He was certainly in danger, but he was so blinded by fear he couldn't recognize I was trying to help him. He bit the hand of his savior. . . .

It is true that animals live by instinct and part of that instinct is the natural fear of man. So, this little critter was just doing what the Lord had programmed him to do: be afraid, run, and fight.

But, it is not so for us. We are told to fear the Lord, yes, but in a healthy way. We are to fear the Lord in the same way that we fear our own mother: we don't wish to disappoint her. Her instructions and wisdom guide us throughout the day and, even when we've done something wrong, we still rush into her arms for a loving hug. We know she will still love us; we know she will always forgive us.

Running from the Lord in fear of our life is a choice. God has not given us a negative spirit of fear, dear one. "For God hath not given us the spirit of fear; but of power, and of love, and of a sound mind" (2 Timothy 1:7).

Sometimes, we are so blinded by fear that we even bite the hand of the Savior. Have you ever been angry with God for your circumstances? Have you ever felt hurt and alone? "Be ye angry, and sin not: let not the sun go down upon your wrath" (Ephesians 4:26).

It's okay to be afraid, and it's okay to be angry. Just make sure your emotions are properly directed. You do have a hunter, and he seeks after your very life. "Be sober, be vigilant; because your adversary the devil, as a roaring lion, walketh about, seeking whom he may devour" (1 Peter 5:8).

Just like my little chipmunk was running for his life from certain doom, as Christians, we can find ourselves doing the same thing. But, the Lord doesn't want us running in fear for our lives. He says to be sober, be vigilant, but above all: *stand!* "Put on the whole armour of God, that ye may be able to stand against the wiles of the devil." (Ephesians 6:11).

Our adversary, the devil, is no insignificant adversary. We should have a healthy respect for him. After all, he's been playing the deceit game for thousands of years and he certainly has our number. We are no match for the devil, and even Michael the Archangel dared not to bring an accusation against him. "Yet Michael the archangel, when contending with the devil he disputed about the body of Moses, durst not bring against him a railing accusation, but said, 'The Lord rebuke thee'" (Jude 1:9).

God does not say to run; He says to stand. And when we do, we do as Michael did: stand fast and release the Lord to fight the battle for us. It is not our battle to fight. We can only fight in natural ways with natural defenses. When we

> Put on the whole armour of God, that ye may be able to stand against the wiles of the devil."
>
> (Ephesians 6:11)

are being attacked spiritually, we need a spirit being to do the fighting for us, and we have that in the form of the Holy Spirit of God.

If you have received Jesus Christ as your personal Savior, the Holy Spirit dwells within you. His job is to fight these battles for you, but you must first release Him into the situation. Let Him do what He's been sent to do: save you! "These things I have spoken unto you, that in me ye might have peace. In the world ye shall have tribulation: but be of good cheer; I have overcome the world" (John 16:33).

Then, we can at last relax, settle our souls, and allow peace and joy to enter again. Let the Lord fight your battles for you, dear one, and simply rest in His loving embrace. Don't choose to writhe and gnash your teeth; His only concern is to save your life.

See the battle for your life as it is: the hunters chasing you, and the Lord scooping you up to help. Invite the Lord Jesus into your life and situation, and then release the Lord into it so that He may save you. Then, rest and be of good cheer as you hear the door shutting on the hunters behind you as you scamper home again in safety.

> "God is a Spirit..."
> (John 4:24)

Notes and Reflections

A One-Sentence Prayer

Chapter 13

Pookie, Tucker, and Hampton

ears ago, my family and I lived in a duplex. The owners were not pet-friendly, so we couldn't have any pets.

I have always been a pet lover; my childhood dream was to become a veterinarian. My poor mother suffered through the saving of countless pets in my youth, including a pigeon named "Pidge." (I giggle now when I think of how I learned to call like a pigeon and spent countless hours "talking" with him.)

When we first moved to the duplex, I had a cat named Pookie. She was a rescue cat that I had found where I used to sit and watch the planes land at the airport. (My father had been a Radar Intercept Officer pilot of an F-4 Phantom—like Goose from *Top Gun*), and I loved the roar of the big engines.) The poor thing was absolutely starving, and on that particular night, I had ordered one too many tacos. She was about six months old, and came running to me when I held out the taco meat, devouring it hungrily and purring loudly. From that moment on, we were inseparable . . .

. . . until we moved into the duplex.

It was an extremely rushed move. We had been given three days' notice to move out of a house that we had been caring for that suddenly underwent a renovation contract. As a young family with a one-year-old daughter, our options were limited to, basically, any housing we could find that was reasonable. We didn't have time to be too picky.

After looking at apartment after apartment in lousy neighborhoods, when I found a sweet,

> "He that hath pity upon the poor lendeth unto the LORD . . ."
> (Proverbs 19:17)

well-cared-for duplex in a good neighborhood, I snatched it right up. I signed the paperwork immediately, without even getting Rob's consent, and went about working on how to surprise him with his new "home." (I knew he'd be thrilled . . . and, thankfully, he was.)

I was left with the problem of what to do with Pookie, however, since there were no pets allowed in the duplex. My Mom graciously agreed to care for her until we moved out, and shortly thereafter, I said goodbye to my beloved kitty as she boarded the plane to Colorado Springs. It would be the last time I saw her.

One night, she escaped from my mother's house, and never came back. My poor mother was heartbroken, and so was I.

So, needless to say, when the duplex came under new management years later, and I found out the owners were pet-friendly, I leapt at the chance to have a kitty again. It was late April by then, and my birthday was April 30. On April 27, I called Rob pleading to get a cat as an early birthday gift. He is not a natural cat-lover, but after some convincing . . . he caved.

That night, the girls and Rob and I loaded up in the car and headed to PetSmart, which has a local adoption center from the Humane Society. By this time, Amanda had joined our family and was about three years old. Samantha was about to turn six. After trying to get some snuggles with some pretty playful kitties, and failing, we came to the last kennel.

The name listed was "Le Pew," a definite negative. *Why would they name a cat that?* I wondered. I looked in the cage to find what may not

> "Delight thyself also in the LORD; and he shall give thee the desires of thine heart."
>
> (Psalms 37:4)

have been described so much as a cat, but a small bear. The grey gently-striped tabby with white socks was enormous. I was not interested in him at all. He wasn't the melt-your-heart cute kitten I had pictured in my mind. This cat was a tank!

But, none of the other cats fit my bill, either. Deciding to look past the stigma of his name, we thought we would see how Le Pew was with the kids. We took him out of the kennel, and he did nothing. And I mean nothing. He simply became a giant sack of gray and white fur as Samantha, Rob, and I passed him back and forth. He didn't move. He didn't resist. He just flopped wherever we put him contentedly. I started to have second thoughts about this ultra-calm kitty.

But, it was when I put him in the lap of our three-year old Amanda that the case for Le Pew was sealed. She wrapped her arms around his belly, and he just sat there, pouring over her lap with all four limbs extended. He didn't flinch one bit. . . .

That was it. This was the cat for us. He may not have been the princess kitty I had dreamed of, but his personality was a *perfect fit*. And so, our big gray cat, Tucker, joined our family. (Incidentally . . . we also found out why he was named Le Pew. As soon as we put him in the car to come home, he lost all control of his bladder. Eeewww . . . and, yup, he's still like that today.)

Nearing October of that same year, Rob's grandmother passed away. We loaded up our car and prepared for the drive from Wisconsin to New York with our two young children.

> "Thou knowest my down-sitting and mine uprising; thou understandest my thought afar off."
>
> (Psalm 139:2)

> "For there is not a word in my ~~tongue~~, but, lo, O LORD, thou knowest it altogether."
>
> (Psalms 139:4)

The day before we left for the funeral, I called my best girlfriend, Liz. We talked about the kids and various other things, as girls tend to do. Somehow, we got onto the subject of me getting another cat. (We were allowed two in the duplex.)

I told Liz that I was going to be very particular this time on the cat I chose. I hadn't bonded with Tucker the way I had hoped to (that came much later), and this time I was going to wait for the perfect cat. As we talked, I launched into descriptive detail on what kind of cat, precisely, I wanted next.

"So, this time, I'm going to wait for my perfect kitty," I said decisively, "It has to be a calico kitty, and it has to be a girl. I want her to have bright white patches of fur, and deep black patches. She should have medium-length fur . . . not too long, but not too short . . . look like a princess . . . and her tail, her tail should be extra long and fluffy. I want her to have little tufts of white hair coming out of her ears . . . and she has to purr like a kitten forever. And she has to love me and be *my* kitty. That would be my perfect kitty, and I'm going to wait until I find her," I told Liz.

Liz chuckled at my laundry list of qualifications, but agreed to keep an eye out for a cat that fit the bill where she lived.

On the return trip home from the funeral, we stopped in Ohio at a Hampton Inn. The girls walked up to the entrance of the hotel ahead of us, and as they neared the door, a flash of white came out from under the bushes toward them. I gasped . . . it was a calico kitten. She looked to be about eleven months old and I stopped dead in my tracks when I saw her. The skittish little kitty darted out from under the bushes to nervously rub her head in the palm of the girls' hands, and then dash away again.

It was so cute to see her stand on her hind legs and thrust her head forward. She eagerly received attentive petting from my girls, and then would run away. And then return. And then run.

Besides being a calico, the next thing I noticed as I began to approach was her loud, rumbling purr. I couldn't believe my eyes and ears...

She was a female.

She was a calico.

Her whites were bright and her darks were dark.

She had medium length fur.

She had an extra-long, fluffy tail.

She looked like a princess.

And to top it all off, she had little white tufts of fur coming out of her ears.

Are you kidding me, Lord? I asked, awe-struck. This was *her*. This was exactly the cat I had described to Liz. Only, this one was starving, riddled with fleas, and very clearly a stray.

Both girls turned to us, with huge, pleading eyes. "Mommy! Daddy! Can we take her home?" they begged.

My heart broke . . . I wanted her, too . . . I mean, how could I say "no" to the kitty of my dreams? But, realistically we were two days away from being home (we had to stop for a meeting in Chicago), and it was a terrible idea to pick up a stray cat on the road. Still, I couldn't help but have my own heart-strings tugged. . . .

> "Such knowledge is too wonderful for me; it is high, I cannot attain unto it." (Psalms 139:6)

> "For ye have not received the spirit of bondage again to fear; but ye have received the Spirit of adoption, whereby we cry, Abba, Father."
>
> (Romans 8:15)

I answered them warmly, "Girls, if the Lord has that cat for us . . . there is no way we're leaving here without her. But, for now, the hotel doesn't take animals and we have to go up to sleep."

Strangely satisfied with that answer, we said goodbye to the skittish little love and headed up to bed.

At breakfast the next morning, the girls piped up, "Mom! Can we see if the kitty is still there and bring her some ham?" Not expecting to see the cat again, I said, "Sure, girls, we can do that."

We stepped outside the hotel and were shocked to see a streak of white fur come running down a hill, across the parking lot, and straight to us . . . her little purr-motor roaring. She ravenously devoured the ham that the girls offered, purring loudly.

That's when they turned on me. . . . "Moooom! Can we keep her?" they asked, eyes wide and pleading. And that's when I turned on Rob. . . .

The poor man. He had all three of his girls looking at him with eyes as big as saucers begging to keep this skittish, starving, flea-bag of a cat. "Please!" we all pleaded.

Then I launched into the cat I had described to Liz, and how I had said if the Lord had this cat for us, we wouldn't leave without her . . . and, and, and . . . *pleeeeeease!*

Rob had no chance. Hanging his head, he conceded defeat. "Okay. We'll keep the cat."

Delighted, I scooped up the kitty, and was shocked at how light and boney she was. Poor baby, I thought . . . no wonder she's so very hungry. She's starving.

We loaded her up in the car, where she slipped my grasp and ran frantic loops around the car, clawing at everything in her path. *Oh, boy, what have we gotten into*, I wondered. On one of her passes by me, I reached out, scooped her up, and put her on her back like a baby in my arms hoping to calm her and keep her still.

She didn't move.

For two whole days in the car, she lay on her back in my arms and wouldn't flinch. We could open the car door and slam it right next to her, and she wouldn't budge.

She knew she was home. She knew she was safe. And we knew that our dear, sweet Hampton had just joined our family. My little dream kitty. . . .

When we arrived home with her, I bathed her and took her immediately to the vet. She was frighteningly skinny, and it was then that we discovered she had a severely broken leg. It was concluded that she must have been run over by a car while living in the parking lot, but the break had healed past the point of being able to fix it.

I can't imagine how this sweet little eleven month old kitten had managed to survive a nearly-severed leg. Yet, somehow she had persevered . . . and I was able to realize that we were just as much her saviors as she was my gift.

She has a little notch out of one ear, and that reminds me of her car accident and the terrible struggle she must have endured. On her mouth, there is a little patch of orange fur that looks like her tongue is hanging out. It reminds me

> "Fear thou not; for I am with thee: be not dismayed; for I am thy God: I will strengthen thee; yea, I will help thee; yea."
>
> (Isaiah 41:10)

> "I will praise the name of God with a song, and will magnify him with thanksgiving."
> (Psalms 69:30)

of how hungry she was. On her left eye, there is a patch of orange fur in the shape of a teardrop. It reminds me how sad and lonely her life had been. . . .

And, every day as my little fluff ball snuggles up with me, purring loudly, my heart swells with gratitude toward the Lord for His perfect little gift.

You know, even though I had been so descriptive about my heart's desire, like most people, I had expected to settle for less. I expected to get eighty percent of what I had hoped for, making some sacrifices for a near-perfect cat in reality. After all, dreams are just dreams, right?

No, actually they're not.

Our God is the God of miracles, and of making the hidden dreams of your heart come true. He calls those things that be not as though they are: "God, who quickeneth the dead, and calleth those things which be not as though they were" (Romans 4:17). In other words, our God is the Alpha and Omega, the beginning and the end, the great "I AM" of both Old and New Testaments. Because of this, He dwells in the eternal present, even though we as humans divide time into the past, present, and future. This is why He knows our thoughts before we think them, our words before we say them, our motives when we can't even figure them out ourselves, and why He can already have set in motion the necessary sequence of events in what we experience as "time" that will result in our "dreams" coming true—in our case, making it possible for Hampton to become part of our family.

He is waiting to prove Himself strong on our

behalf: "For the eyes of the LORD run to and fro throughout the whole earth, to shew himself strong in the behalf of them whose heart is perfect toward him" (2 Chronicles 16:9).

He gives us the desires of our hearts: "Delight thyself also in the LORD; and he shall give thee the desires of thine heart" (Psalms 37:4).

He wants to pour out a blessing we cannot contain: "Prove me now herewith, saith the LORD of hosts, if I will not open you the windows of heaven, and pour you out a blessing, that there shall not be room enough to receive it" (Malachi 3:10).

And He is able to do it: "Now unto him that is able to do exceeding abundantly above all that we ask or think . . ." (Ephesians 3:20).

What is it your heart wishes for today? Have you committed it to the Lord? If your heart's desire lines up with the will of God, there is nothing that can stand in the way of your receiving it.

Do you believe He can do it?

Are you willing to believe He will?

When a simple white streak of blessing appears in your life, make sure you commit it to Him. Rest in the Lord, knowing that: If God has that little kitty for you, there is no way you're leaving here without her. Then, simply scoop up your blessing and say "Father, thanks. . . ."

> "For with God nothing shall be impossible."
> (Luke 1:37)

Notes and Reflections

A One-Sentence Prayer

Chapter 14

Elijah, the Widow, and Giving

In 1 Kings 17, the prophet Elijah is on the run. The evil King Ahab had done more to provoke the Lord to wrath than all of the kings of Israel before him, including raising an altar to worship Baal. The Lord spoke through Elijah saying that there would not be rain or dew upon the land except by his word.

He threatened famine, and Ahab sough to destroy him. So, the Lord commanded him to go to the brook Cherith. For a time, God cared for Elijah by bringing him food by the mouth of the ravens.

There was no rain during those days, as Elijah had said, and eventually the brook dried up. As thirst set in, the Lord moved him on.

He told Elijah to rise up and go to Zarephath, having commanded a widow woman there to care for him. So, Elijah went.

When he came upon the widow in her field, the story takes a poignant turn.

The woman's face is drawn as he watches her gather sticks. He is terribly thirsty, and Elijah calls out, *"Fetch me, I pray thee, a little water in a vessel, that I may drink."*

She turned to fetch him a cup of water, and as she left, he called out to her again. *"Bring me, I pray thee, a morsel of bread in thine hand."*

The widow had a defeated look on her face as she quietly replied, *"As the LORD thy God liveth, I have not a cake, but an handful of meal in a barrel, and a little oil in a cruse: and, behold, I am gathering two sticks, that I may go in and dress it for me and my son, that we may eat it, and die."*

Elijah was witnessing the woman gathering

> "Be content with such things as ye have: for he hath said, I will never leave thee, nor forsake thee."
> (Hebrews 13:5)

sticks to build a small fire to cook her last meal. Her resources had run out . . . she was at the end of herself. With only a handful of meal left, she knew she and her son would die the slow and terrible death of starvation.

Strangely, Elijah said to her, *"Fear not; go and do as thou hast said: but make me thereof a little cake first, and bring it unto me, and after make for thee and for thy son."*

Can you imagine? This was her last meal, and instead of rising up to fix her problems, Elijah actually asked her to feed him *first*.

Talk about abject poverty . . . this woman told Elijah that she and her son would eat and then die of starvation. Elijah understood what kind of situation she was in, and yet *he insisted she give to him first.* "Oh, you and your son are starving and going to die after you've eaten that last little cake? Well, you should give to me first."

Our natural instincts tell us to say, "She and her son need it . . . it's all they have . . . Elijah may be hungry, but he shouldn't take their last morsel of meal! That would be too selfish!" But, this story is not about Elijah. It's about the widow, and bringing her to a deeper understanding of faith in the Lord.

Elijah then makes a promise, *"For thus saith the LORD God of Israel, The barrel of meal shall not waste, neither shall the cruse of oil fail, until the day that the LORD sendeth rain upon the earth."*

Like the widow and the Little Pot of Oil, she walked away with nothing but the word of God. Thankfully, like our widow in the Little Pot of Oil, she chose to act in faith. *"And she went and*

> "Give, and it shall be given unto you; good measure, pressed down, and shaken together, and running over . . ."
>
> (Luke 6:38)

did according to the saying of Elijah: and she, and he, and her house, did eat many days. And the barrel of meal wasted not, neither did the cruse of oil fail, according to the word of the LORD, which he spake by Elijah."

But, the story doesn't end there . . .

"And it came to pass after these things, that the son of the woman, the mistress of the house, fell sick; and his sickness was so sore, that there was no breath left in him."

Sadly, her son dies from illness. In the widow's distress, she presses Elijah.

"What have I to do with thee, O thou man of God? Art thou come unto me to call my sin to remembrance, and to slay my son?"

She can't understand why the prophet would save her life only to slay her son for her sins.

"And he cried unto the LORD, and said, O LORD my God, hast thou also brought evil upon the widow with whom I sojourn, by slaying her son?"

"And the LORD heard the voice of Elijah; and the soul of the child came into him again, and he revived. And Elijah took the child, and brought him down out of the chamber into the house, and delivered him unto his mother: and Elijah said, See, thy son liveth. And the woman said to Elijah, Now by this I know that thou art a man of God, and that the word of the LORD in thy mouth is truth."

If Elijah had refused to partake of their last handful of meal, they would have died of starvation. Instead, because they gave out of their poverty, the woman and her son were exceedingly blessed.

Not only did it save the life of the mother and son, but it brought them into fellowship with

> "For as the Father raiseth up the dead, and quickeneth them; even so the Son quickeneth whom he will."
>
> (John 5:21)

the Lord which saved the life of the son yet another time. She gave a little meal, and her house was filled with food and oil, and four lives were saved because of it (Elijah's, the widow's, and the son twice). Talk about a proof text for "give and it shall be given unto you."

We have to know in our hearts that the Lord is faithful to His word, and will increase the giver as promised. Life or death. Blessing or cursing. Increase or decrease. It's up to us, the receivers.

> "But this I say, He which soweth sparingly shall reap also sparingly; and he which soweth bountifully shall reap also bountifully. Every man according as he purposeth in his heart, so let him give; not grudgingly, or of necessity: for God loveth a cheerful giver. And God is able to make all grace abound toward you; that ye, always having all sufficiency in all things, may abound to every good work . . ." (2 Corinthians 9:6-8).

If the Lord puts something on the heart of the giver, we are commanded to give accordingly. Not "of necessity" when we *have* to give because it's expected or required, but just because the Lord has put it on our hearts to give for whatever reason.

> "Withhold not good from them to whom it is due, when it is in the power of thine hand to do it. Say not unto thy neighbour, 'Go, and come again, and to morrow I will give'; when thou hast it by thee" (Prov. 3:27-30).

"God loveth a cheerful giver."
(2 Corinthians 9:7)

Elijah, the Widow, and Giving

Was the widow *able* to give the meal? Yes, it was hers to give. She possessed it; she could give it. Does that Scripture say "give only what we can afford to give"? No, that would contradict both of the widow stories I shared with you. If you have it—give it, according to the Lord. If you own $2, then you are physically able to give it away. If you don't, you can't.

What would the widow's friends have thought of her when she chose to give her last handful of meal to Elijah first instead of her own child? Think they would have counseled her against it? Sure, they would have . . . but, their logical reasoning on how she couldn't afford it, and that her family needed it more, would have ultimately killed her, her son, and Elijah, too. She was given direct instructions by the Lord, and in her obedience to Him, she was saved by giving even when she thought she couldn't afford to.

Sometimes we think, "I want to, but I just can't afford to give," while the Lord says: "You can't afford *not* to give."

We may want to say, "My friend can't afford to give that! I can't accept this!" while the Lord says: "*They* can't afford for you not to receive this. They need the blessing, and I want to bless them back."

Just like the Lord Jesus did, all God wants you to do is lift up your heart to Him and say: "Father, thanks. . . ."

In turn, He will simply reply: "Christian, thanks. *I'll take it from here.* . . ."

> "The righteous giveth and spareth not."
> (Proverbs 21:26)

Notes and Reflections

A One-Sentence Prayer

Chapter 15

Consider the Lily

It was a cold, crisp night in Chicago. I was a cosmetic dental assistant travelling for a seminar on aesthetic dentistry. My daughters were young (about six and three) and my first priority was to find souvenirs for them. I was accompanied by my doctor, who was also my pastor at the time.

I had heard of the "Magnificent Mile" in Chicago, and was eager to shop until I dropped, or at least until the time came for our dinner reservations at the renowned Chophouse. We talked casually of the upcoming seminar as we strolled the buzzing streets of Chicago, window shopping.

When I saw the bright colors of The Disney Store beckoning to me, I carefully picked my way over to the store, watchful for the heavy traffic. Christmastime was approaching, and the doctor left in search of a gift for his wife at Ralph Lauren.

I scoured the store for the perfect gifts for my girls, and finally found a Princess Aurora nightgown for Samantha (her favorite princess), and a Tinker Bell nightgown for Amanda (who loves green). Once I completed my purchase, I headed out to Starbucks to meet back up with the doctor.

I ordered my favorite Venti Vanilla Latte with an extra shot of espresso, and a bit of whipped cream. Once my piping hot, bittersweet drink was in my hands, we began to work our way back to the car.

The streets were brimming with life and activity. Cars honked as cabs weaved in and out of traffic. Groups of giggling girls passed, talking excitedly. Families held hands as they strolled

> "Every man is a friend to him that giveth gifts."
> (Proverbs 19:6)

> "Open thine hand wide unto thy brother, to thy poor, and to thy needy, in thy land."
>
> (Deuteronomy 15:11)

the sidewalks.

We came to an intersection where the light was red, and waited patiently for the "walk" sign to cross. As we waited, I noticed an older woman crossing toward us. She was dark-skinned and her ragged appearance spoke of a hard life.

She asked the gentleman in front of me if he had any change to spare. "No," was his quick answer.

I knew she would work her way over to me next, and my mind scrambled with how to answer her. I had spent my last five dollars on the coffee I was holding in my hand, a luxury I was suddenly acutely aware of.

She walked toward me with slight limp and her back was stooped from age. Her thick, wiry hair was unkempt and stuck out everywhere in unwashed clumps. It was parted in the middle, and two streaks of silver-white hair led me to believe she was in her mid-sixties.

She had many layers of dirty, drab clothes on, and a blanket on top of them. Her dark, fingerless gloves were tattered and torn, with strands of weathered yarn hanging from them. Everything about her said she was homeless and alone.

"Do you have any spare change?" came her shaky voice as she looked at me with pleading eyes.

My heart broke knowing I had nothing to give her. *Lord, what have I to give this child of yours?*

Softly, the childhood hymn, "Silver and Gold Have I None," drifted across my mind: *but such as I have give I thee . . .*

"Oh, honey," I said tenderly, putting my hand

Consider the Lily

on her arm, "the only thing I have to offer you is the Kingdom of Heaven."

"Oh," she gasped, her eyes welling with tears, "Oh, how could I ask for more than that?"

My heart leapt for joy for her imminent salvation, and I began to tremble. Suddenly at a loss for words, I called to the doctor.

"Pastor?" I called out, "she would like to receive the Lord."

He turned around and walked over to where we stood on the corner of the sidewalk.

How many people had rejected this woman? How many times had she heard the word "no"? I wondered silently, *How many had taunted and spit at her?*

Huddled together for warmth and privacy, we began the gentle process of leading her to Christ.

"My dear friend, do you know you are a sinner?" Pastor asked her.

"Oh, yes, *yes* . . ." she replied brokenly, with hot tears streaming down her plump cheeks.

He continued, "We have all sinned before God, and our sins have penalties associated with them. The wages of sin is death, dear one. But, the good news is that Jesus died to pay your sin debt in its entirety. He has promised to pay the whole of your debt—if you are willing to receive it. When you do, every bad thing you have ever said or done is covered perfectly by the blood of the Lord Jesus Christ. Your sins are cast as far as the east is from the west, and God promises not to remember them anymore.

Do you believe that Jesus died to pay for your sins?" He asked, with a hand on her shoulder.

> "And he said unto them, Go ye into all the world, and preach the gospel to every creature."
> (Mark 16:15)

> "Behold, I stand at the door, and knock: if any man hear my voice, and open the door, I will come in to him, and will sup with him, and he with me."
>
> (Revelation 3:20)

"Yes, oh, Lord knows I do!" she cried.

"Are you ready to receive your gift of eternal life in the Kingdom of Heaven?"

"Yes, I am," she sputtered, *"please!"*

I leaned in to her, and said in gentle tones, "Then repeat after me. Lord Jesus, I believe I am a sinner for whom you died. . . .

Thank you, Lord for paying my sin debt . . . I now receive you into my life and accept your gift of eternal salvation . . .

In Jesus' name, I pray, Amen."

She faithfully repeated the prayer with a humble heart, truly ready to receive the Lord, and choking emotionally on the words.

"Darling sister," I said warmly, "your home is now in Heaven, and when you die you will have a glorious mansion on a street paved with gold. The Lord promises he will never—*ever*—leave you nor forsake you," I said as I hugged her close, ignoring the smell.

She hugged me back, sobbing, "Thank you, oh, thank you . . ."

I pressed my coffee into her hand, the only thing I had to offer, and said "Here, this is for you. It's a taste of your new life and all of the treasures of Heaven."

Pastor handed her $20, "and this is for you, too."

"Never forget . . . you are a child of the King now, dear sister," I said, putting my hand on her cheek. I kissed her forehead just as the light turned green for us to cross. She walked away, shaking and crying for joy, and we turned to cross the street.

This beautiful soul who had approached us

with nothing, walked away with a Starbucks, $20, and the keys to the Kingdom of Heaven itself. Once just a beggar, she was now the daughter of the King. Once just a stranger, she was now my sister in Christ.

"Lily," said Pastor. "We shall call her Lily...because you stopped to consider her in the light of God's glory."

"Consider the lilies," I said, quoting Luke 12:27, "Yes, Lily . . ."

As we stepped off the curb, the first glittering flakes of snow began to fall. *My favorite kind of snow . . . thank you, Lord,* I prayed inwardly, *I love it when you make the world sparkle.*

Well done, thou good and faithful servant, came His gentle reply.

How often do we judge the worthiness of another by their outward appearance? How many times have we prejudged a soul's willingness to receive Christ? Will you be as the man who turned her away, or as the one who helped lead her to Christ?

Who is it you feel you can't help? Where do you feel your human strength has failed you?

As long you are focusing on yourself and what you have to offer, you are bound to fail. It is only when you have come to the end of yourself, and have nothing left to offer but Christ Himself that the Lord will faithfully pour through you.

Such as I have give I thee . . .

For it is then that you will finally lift your heart to the Lord, desperately pleading and ask, *Lord, what do I have to give to her?*

To which the Lord will reply: *Consider the Lily. . . .*

> "Silver and gold have I none; but such as I have give I thee . . ."
>
> (Acts 3:6)

Notes and Reflections

A One-Sentence Prayer

Chapter 16

God Loves You Circle

As my mother-in-law was dying of lung cancer years ago, one of her final wishes was to get a hope necklace for me and my sister-in-law. It was a simple white gold circle with inset diamonds on a white gold chain. It was beautiful.

The day I received it was a poignant day in my life for a couple of reasons. First, it would be the last time I would see my mother in law alive, and secondly because of the profound insight my five-year-old daughter, Amanda, would soon share with me.

As I drove my daughters home from visiting Hospice Care, I was absent-mindedly fingering the necklace. My thoughts drifted to our own mortality and my heart swelled with love and appreciation for the precious lives of my children in the back seat.

I wondered how much my five- and eight-year-old daughters truly understood the tough days we were facing.

As we drove along the beautiful country roads, the sun was setting and a golden wash of sunlight caught the diamonds in the necklace. Gentle streams of light refracted through the necklace and cast dancing lights on the roof of the car.

Amanda, my five-year-old, suddenly asked, "Mommy?"

"Yes, love?" I replied.

In her sweet, lilting voice she asked, "Why is your necklace a circle?"

I paused a moment . . .

"I suppose it's because circles have no beginning and no end; it's a symbol of hope," I replied gently.

> "Out of the mouth of babes . . . hast thou ordained strength."
> (Psalms 8:2)

> "The LORD hath appeared of old unto me, saying, Yea, I have loved thee with an everlasting love."
> (Jeremiah 31:3)

After a moment, she said timidly, "Momma?"

"Yes?" I encouraged.

"I love you circle, because that never ends," she said simply.

I will never forget that moment . . .

In the midst of a dark and terrible time, here was my sweet daughter saying some of the loveliest words I'd ever heard.

And I saw the Lord in them . . .

We all have hard days. Some are harder than others but, through it all, the Lord's love for us is constant. It is unwavering; it is endless.

No matter how distant He may seem, the circle of love which encompasses us can never be broken. We cannot understand the beginning of it, and we cannot fathom the end of it.

We are hid in the hand of Jesus, and Jesus is hid in the hand of the Father, and nothing—not one thing—can pry us out of that circle of protective love.

When you are at your lowest of lows, feeling lonelier than ever, and facing hardships you've never imagined . . . never forget:

God loves you circle, because that never ends.

Notes and Reflections

A One-Sentence Prayer

Meet the Johnsons

We are quirky and fun, serious and creative, and most of all . . . we are loving and Christian.

My eldest daughter, Samantha, is a gentle and sweet soul. At age 14, her flowing golden brown hair cascades around her shoulders in gentle waves and curls, framing a beautiful, heart-shaped face. Her bright blue eyes shine forth atop her soft, dusty rose cheekbones, and speak volumes of the precious soul beneath.

She is brilliantly creative with a true gift for composing beautiful piano pieces. When sitting at the piano, she would much rather play from her soul than read sheet music (which she can also do quite well). She plays flute, drums, saxophone, and a little guitar, too. She is a writer, an artist, a dreamer, and a thinker. Her name means "The Listener of God" and she is truly that.

Samantha is quiet and reserved, yet confident and strong. Sometimes, it can be hard to get her to start talking, but, oh boy . . . once you do . . . be ready for an extremely detailed conversation. I smile when I listen to her. She is so verbally descriptive that it makes you feel as if you were right there with her every step of the way. She is a walking verbal picture book.

Samantha is her own lovely person, but shares some particularly endearing traits with my husband, Rob, and me. She looks exactly like me, but thinks exactly like him. I am the musical one in our family, but she has a particular fondness for electronics and engineering like my husband. She is a beautiful amalgamation of the two of us with her own perfectly wonderful individuality.

She is strong in her faith, solid and true. She loves the Lord, she loves her Momma, she loves her sister . . . but her heart truly belongs to Daddy.

Amanda, at age 11, is our package of personality. Her short, fine medium-brown hair is straight, framing her strikingly beautiful features. Her high cheek bones support her stylish glasses, bringing out her deep gray-blue eyes. She is slender and elegant, with long, graceful arms and legs. Her name means "Beloved of God," and she lives up to every ounce of it.

Amanda is a ball of fun-loving, creative energy. She is already an amazing pianist and prefers reading sheet music over composition, although she has composed beautiful pieces. She has recently picked up flute, and has astonished me (a flute teacher) at her depth of tonal quality. She has a truly gifted ear for making a perfect tone, complete with a gentle vibrato.

Amanda may be the talker when others are around, but spends most of her time quiet. Where Samantha will walk me through her entire day at school, Amanda's answer to "Tell me about your day," is usually, "It was fine. Nothing big." She is the life of the party in public, but needs to be drawn out at home.

She is confident and well-poised, and has a natural gift for public speaking and performance. She is extremely solid in her faith, and has a passion for evangelism, having even led adults to the Lord. She and I share so many personality traits that we often call her "Mini-me." She is fun, creative, happy, and always crafting something big.

In September, you will find her in front of the fireplace, knitting a scarf quietly, with Christmas music softly playing and scented candles burning. Her socks are fun and funky, and her style uniquely her.

She is an absolute treasure, and adds joy to everyone's day. We call her my little "lap dog" as she can usually be found snuggling with me. She loves the Lord, she loves her Daddy, she loves her sister . . . but her heart truly belongs to Momma.

Rob is a truly godly husband and father. He is gentle and kind, but a strong and confident leader. A graduate of West Point and a former Army Airborne Ranger, Rob is the man to lead men. His unique gift to find a simple solution to every problem has promoted him far in life.

A man of true character, who deeply loves his family, Rob's reputation precedes him everywhere he goes. His number one priority in life is his family, and he lives by it daily. He is an amazing public speaker, and occasionally preaches at church. He is tall, handsome, and the love of my life. . . .

~ *Michelle Johnson*

Resources from Healthy Life Press

Unless otherwise noted on the site itself, shipping is free for all products purchased through www.healthylifepress.com.

We've Got Mail: The New Testament Letters in Modern English – As Relevant Today as Ever! by Rev. Warren C. Biebel, Jr. – A modern English paraphrase of the New Testament Letters, sure to inspire in readers a loving appreciation for God's Word. (Printed book: $9.95; PDF eBook: $6.95; both together: $15.00, direct from publisher; eBook reader versions available at www.Amazon.com; www.BN.com; www.eChristian.com.)

Hearth & Home – Recipes for Life, by Karey Swan (7th Edition) – Far more than a cookbook, this classic is a life book, with recipes for life as well as for great food. Karey describes how to buy and prepare from scratch a wide variety of tantalizing dishes, while weaving into the book's fabric the wisdom of the ages plus the recipe that  she and her husband used to raise their kids. A great gift for Christmas or for a new bride. (Perfect Bound book [8 x 10, glossy cover]: $17.95; PDF eBook: $12.95; both together: $24.95, direct from publisher; eBook reader versions available at www.Amazon.com; www.BN.com; www.eChristian.com.)

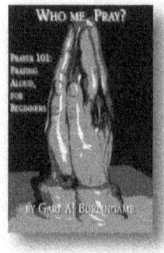

Who Me, Pray? Prayer 101: Praying Aloud, for Beginners, by Gary A. Burlingame – *Who Me, Pray?* is a practical guide for prayer, based on Jesus' direction in "The Lord's Prayer," with examples provided for use in typical situations where you might be asked or expected to pray in public. (Printed book: $6.95; PDF eBook: $2.99; both together: $7.95, direct from publisher; eBook reader versions available at www.Amazon.com; www.BN.com; www.eChristian.com.)

The Big Black Book – What the Christmas Tree Saw, by Rev. Warren C. Biebel, Jr. – An original Christmas story, from the perspective of the Christmas tree. This little book is especially suitable for parents to read to their children at Christmas time or all year-round. (Full-color printed book: $9.95; PDF eBook: $4.95; both together: $10.95, direct from publisher; eBook reader versions available at www.Amazon.com; www.BN.com; www.eChristian.com.)

My Broken Heart Sings, the poetry of Gary Burlingame – In 1987, Gary and his wife Debbie lost their son Christopher John, at only six months of age, to a chronic lung disease. This life-changing experience gave them a special heart for helping others through similar loss and pain. (Printed book: $10.95; PDF eBook: $6.95; both together: $13.95; eBook reader versions available at www.Amazon.com; www.BN.com; www.eChristian.com.)

After Normal: One Teen's Journey Following Her Brother's Death, by Diane Aggen – Based on a journal the author kept following her younger brother's death. It offers helpful insights and understanding for teens facing a similar loss or for those who might wish to understand and help teens facing a similar loss. (Printed book: $11.95; PDF eBook: $6.95; both together: $15.00; eBook reader versions available at www.Amazon.com; www.BN.com; www.eChristian.com.)

In the Unlikely Event of a Water Landing – Lessons Learned from Landing in the Hudson River, by Andrew Jamison, MD – The author was flying standby on US Airways Flight 1549 toward Charlotte on January 15, 2009, from New York City, where he had been interviewing for a residency position. Little did he know that the next stop would be the Hudson River. Riveting and inspirational, this

book would be especially helpful for people in need of hope and encouragement. (Printed book: $8.95; PDF eBook: $6.95; both together: $12.95, direct from publisher; eBook reader versions available at www.Amazon.com; www.BN.com; www.eChristian.com.)

Finding Martians in the Dark – Everything I Needed to Know About Teaching Took Me Only 30 Years to Learn, by Dan M. Biebel – Packed with wise advice based on hard experience, and laced with humor, this book is a perfect teacher's gift year-round. Susan J. Wegmann, PhD, says, "Biebel's sardonic wit is mellowed by a genuine love for kids and teaching. . . . A Whitman-like sensibility flows through his stories of teaching, learning, and life." (Printed book: $10.95; PDF eBook: $6.95; Together: $15.00; eBook reader versions available at www.Amazon.com; www.BN.com; www.eChristian.com.)

Because We're Family and **Because We're Friends**, by Gary A. Burlingame – Sometimes things related to faith can be hard to discuss with your family and friends. These booklets are designed to be given as gifts, to help you open the door to discussing spiritual matters with family members and friends who are open to such a conversation. (Printed book: $5.95 each; PDF eBook: $4.95 each; both together: $9.95 [printed & eBook of the same title], direct from publisher; eBook reader versions available at www.Amazon.com; www.BN.com; www.eChristian.com.)

The Transforming Power of Story: How Telling Your Story Brings Hope to Others and Healing to Yourself, by Elaine Leong Eng, MD, and David B. Biebel, DMin – This book demonstrates, through multiple true life stories, how sharing one's story, especially in a group setting, can bring hope to listeners and healing to the one who shares. Individuals facing difficulties will find this book greatly encouraging. (Printed book: $14.99; PDF eBook: $9.99; both together: $19.99, direct from publisher; eBook reader versions available at www.Amazon.com; www.BN.com; www.eChristian.com.)

You Deserved a Better Father: Good Parenting Takes a Plan, by Robb Brandt, MD – About parenting by intention, and other lessons the author learned through the loss of his firstborn son. It is especially for parents who believe that bits and pieces of leftover time will be enough for their own children. (Printed book: $12.95 each; PDF eBook: $6.95; both together: $17.95, direct from the publisher; eBook reader versions available at www.Amazon.com; www.BN.com; www.eChristian.com.)

Jonathan, You Left Too Soon, by David B. Biebel, DMin – One pastor's journey through the loss of his son, into the darkness of depression, and back into the light of joy again, emerging with a renewed sense of mission. (Printed book: $12.95; PDF eBook: $5.99; both together: $15.00, direct from publisher; eBook reader versions available at www.Amazon.com; www.BN.com; www.eChristian.com.)

The Spiritual Fitness Checkup for the 50-Something Woman, by Sharon V. King, PhD – Following the stages of a routine medical exam, the author describes ten spiritual fitness "checkups" midlife women can conduct to assess their spiritual health and tone up their relationship with God. Each checkup consists of the author's personal reflections, a Scripture reference for meditation, and a "Spiritual Pulse Check," with exercises readers can use for personal application. (Printed book: $8.95; PDF eBook: $6.95; both together: $12.95, direct from publisher; eBook reader versions available at www.Amazon.com; www.BN.com; www.eChristian.com.)

**The Other Side of Life – Over 60? God Still Has a Plan for You**, by Rev. Warren C. Biebel, Jr. – Drawing on biblical examples and his 60-plus years of pastoral experience, Rev. Biebel helps older (and younger) adults understand God's view of aging and the rich life available to everyone who seeks a deeper relationship with God as they age. Rev. Biebel explains how to: Identify God's ongoing plan for your life; Rely on faith to manage the anxieties of aging; Form positive, supportive relationships; Cultivate patience; Cope with new technologies; Develop spiritual integrity; Understand the effects of dementia; Develop a Christ-centered perspective of aging. (Printed book: $10.95; PDF eBook: $6.95; both together: $15.00, direct from publisher; eBook reader versions available at www.Amazon.com; www.BN.com; www.eChristian.com.)

My Faith, My Poetry, by Gary A. Burlingame – This unique book of Christian poetry is actually two in one. The first collection of poems, *A Day in the Life*, explores a working parent's daily journey of faith. The reader is carried from morning to bedtime, from "In the Details," to "I Forgot to Pray," back to "Home Base," and finally to "Eternal Love Divine." The second collection of  poems, *Come Running*, is wonder, joy, and faith wrapped up in words that encourage and inspire the mind and the heart. (Printed book: $10.95; PDF eBook: $6.95; both together: $13.95, direct from publisher; eBook reader versions available at www.Amazon.com; www.BN.com; www.eChristian.com.)

**On Eagles' Wings,** by Sara Eggleston – One woman's life journey from idyllic through chaotic to joy, carried all the way by the One who has promised to never leave us nor forsake us. Remarkable, poignant, moving, and inspiring, this autobiographical account will help many who are facing difficulties that seem too great to overcome or even bear at all. It is proof that Isaiah 40:31 is as true today as when it was penned, "But they that wait upon the

LORD shall renew their strength; they shall mount up with wings as eagles; they shall run, and not be weary; and they shall walk, and not faint." (Printed book: $14.95; PDF eBook: $8.95; both together: $22.95, direct from publisher; eBook reader versions available at www.Amazon.com; www.BN.com; www.eChristian.com.)

Richer Descriptions, by Gary A. Burlingame – A unique and handy manual, covering all <u>nine</u> human senses in seven chapters, for Christian speakers and writers. Exercises and a speaker's checklist equip speakers to engage their audiences in a richer experience. Writing examples and a writer's guide help writers bring more life to the characters and scenes of their stories. Bible references encourage a deeper appreciation of being created by God for a sensory existence. (Printed book: $15.95; PDF eBook: $8.95; both together: $22.95, direct from publisher; eBook reader versions available at www.Amazon.com; www.BN.com; www.eChristian.com.)

Treasuring Grace, by Rob Plumley and Tracy Roberts – This novel was inspired by a dream. Liz Swanson's life isn't quite what she'd imagined, but she considers herself lucky. She has a good husband, beautiful children, and fulfillment outside of her home through volunteer work. On some days she doesn't even notice the dull ache in her heart. While she's preparing for their summer  kickoff at Lake George, the ache disappears and her sudden happiness is mistaken for anticipation of their weekend. However, as the family heads north, there are clouds on the horizon that have nothing to do with the weather. Only Liz's daughter, who's found some of her mother's hidden journals, has any idea what's wrong. But by the end of the weekend, there will be no escaping the truth or its painful buried secrets. (Printed: $12.95; PDF eBook: $7.95; both together: $19.95, direct from publisher; eBook reader versions available at www.Amazon.com; www.BN.com; www.eChristian.com.)

Life's A Symphony, by Mary Z. Smith – When Kate Spence Cooper receives the news that her husband, Jack, has been killed in the war, she and her young son Jeremy move back to Crawford Wood, Tennessee to be closer to family. Since Jack's death Kate feels that she's lost trust in everyone, including God. Will she ever find her way back to the only One whom she can always depend upon? And what about Kate's match making brother, Chance? The cheeky man has other ideas on how to bring happiness into his sister's life once more. (Printed book: $12.95; PDF eBook: $7.95; both together: $19.95, direct from publisher; eBook reader versions available at www.Amazon.com; www.BN.com; www.eChristian.com.)

Your Mind at Its Best – 40 Ways To Keep Your Brain Sharp, by David B. Biebel, DMin; James E. Dill, MD; and, Bobbie Dill, RN – Everyone wants their mind to function at high levels throughout life. In 40 easy-to-understand chapters, readers will discover a wide variety of tips and tricks to keep their minds sharp. Synthesizing science and self-help, *Your Mind at Its Best* makes fascinating neurological discoveries understandable and immediately applicable to readers of any age. (Printed book: $13.99.)

From Orphan to Physician – The Winding Path, by Chun-Wai Chan, MD – From the foreword: "In this book, Dr. Chan describes how his family escaped to Hong Kong, how they survived in utter poverty, and how he went from being an orphan to graduating from Harvard Medical School and becoming a cardiologist. The writing is fluent, easy to read and understand. The sequence of events is realistic, emotionally moving, spiritually touching, heartwarming, and thought provoking. The book illustrates . . . how one must have faith in order to walk through life's winding path." (Printed book: $14.95; PDF eBook: $8.95; both together: $22.95, direct from publisher; eBook reader versions available at www.Amazon.com; www.BN.com; www.eChristian.com.)

12 Parables, by Wayne Faust – Timeless Christian stories about doubt, fear, change, grief, and more. Using tight, entertaining prose, professional musician and comedy performer Wayne Faust manages to deal with difficult concepts in a simple, straightforward way. These are stories you can read aloud over and over—to your spouse, your family, or in a group setting. Packed with emotion and just enough mystery to keep you wondering, while providing lots of points to ponder and discuss when you're through, these stories relate the gospel in the tradition of the greatest speaker of parables the world has ever known, who appears in them often. (Printed book: $14.95; PDF eBook: $8.95; both together: $22.95, direct from publisher; eBook reader versions available at www.Amazon.com; www.BN.com; www.eChristian.com.)

The Answer is Always "Jesus," by Aram Haroutunian, who gave children's sermons for 15 years at a large church in Golden, Colorado— well over 500 in all. This book contains 74 of his most unforgettable presentations—due to the children's responses. Pastors, homeschoolers, parents who often lead family devotions, or other storytellers will find these stories, along with  comments about props and how to prepare and present them, an invaluable asset in reconnecting with the simplest, most profound truths of Scripture, and then to envision how best to communicate these so even a child can understand them. (Printed book: $12.95; PDF eBook: $8.95; both together: $19.95, direct from publisher; eBook reader versions available at www.Amazon.com; www.BN.com; www.eChristian.com.)

Handbook of Faith, by Rev. Warren C. Biebel, Jr. – The *New York Times World 2011 Almanac* claimed that there are 2 billion, 200 thousand Christians in the world, with "Christians" being defined as "followers of Christ." The original 12 followers of Christ changed the world; indeed, they changed the history of the world. So this author, a pastor with over 60 years' experience, poses and answers this logical question: "If there are so many 'Christians' on this planet, why are they so relatively ineffective in serving the One they claim to follow?" Answer: Because, unlike Him, they do not know and trust the Scriptures, implicitly. This little volume will help you do that. (Printed book: $8.95; PDF eBook: $6.95; both together: $13.95, direct from publisher; eBook reader versions available at www.Amazon.com; www.BN.com; www.eChristian.com.)

Pieces of My Heart, by David L. Wood – Eighty-two lessons from normal everyday life. David's hope is that these stories will spark thoughts about God's constant involvement and intervention in our lives and stir a sense of how much He cares about every detail that is important to us. The piece missing represents his son, Daniel, who died in a fire shortly before his first birthday. (Printed book: $16.95; PDF eBook: $8.95; both together: $24.95, direct from publisher; eBook reader versions available at www.Amazon.com; www.BN.com; www.eChristian.com.)

◆ PLEASE NOTE:

Prices listed in this catalog may have been updated since these pages were printed. Current prices are indicated on our website: *www.healthylifepress.com*. Individuals or retail outlets that wish more information may contact us at: *info@healthylifepress.com*.

Dream House, by Justa Carpenter – Written by a New England builder of several hundred homes, the idea for this book came to him one day as he was driving that came to him one day as was driving from one job site to another. He pulled over and recorded it so he would remember it, and now you will remember it, too, if you believe, as he

does, that ". . . He who has begun a good work in you will complete it until the day of Jesus Christ." (Printed book: $8.95; PDF eBook: $6.95; both together: $13.95, direct from publisher; eBook reader versions available at www.Amazon.com; www.BN.com; www.eChristian.com.)

A Simply Homemade Clean, by homesteader Lisa Barthuly – "Somewhere along the path, it seems we've lost our gumption, the desire to make things ourselves," says the author. "Gone are the days of 'do it yourself.' Really . . . why bother? There are a slew of retailers just waiting for us with anything and everything we could need; packaged up all pretty, with no thought or effort required. It is the manifestation of 'progress' . . . right?" I don't buy that!" Instead, Lisa describes how to make safe and effective cleansers for home, laundry, and body right in your own home. This saves money and avoids exposure to harmful chemicals often found in commercially produced cleansers. (Printed book: $12.99; PDF eBook: $6.95; both together: $17.95, direct from publisher; **full-color printed book: $16.99**, only at www.healthylifepress.com; eBook reader versions available at www.Amazon.com; www.BN.com; www.eChristian.com.)

HEALTHY LIFE PRESS DISTRIBUTION

Most Healthy Life Press books are available worldwide online and through bookstores. Distribution is primarily through CreateSpace.com. Bookstores may order at a discount directly from the publisher. For details, e-mail us at: info@healthylifepress.com. Our ePublications are available through _Amazon.com_ (Kindle), _BN.com_ (Nook), and for all commercial readers through _eChristian.com_. All resources are available via *www.healthylifepress.com*.

Recommended Resources – Pro-Life DVD Series

See WWW.HEALTHYLIFEPRESS.COM (select "DVD")
for Trailers and Special Combination Pricing

Eyewitness 2 (Public School Version) – This DVD has been used in many public schools. It is a fascinating journey through 38 weeks of pregnancy, showing developing babies via cutting edge digital ultrasound technology. Separate chapters allow viewing distinct segments individually. (List Price: $34.95; Sale Price: $24.95.)

Window To The Womb (2 DVD Disc Set) Disc 1: Ian Donald (1910-1987) "A Prophetic Legacy;" Disc 2: "A Journey from Death To Life" (50 min) – Includes history of sonography and its increasing impact against abortion—more than 80% of expectant parents who "see" their developing baby choose for life. Perfect for counseling and education in Pregnancy Centers, Christian schools, homeschools, and churches. (List: $49.95; Sale: $34.95.)

Window To the Womb (Pregnancy Care & Counseling Version) – Facts about fetal development, abortion complications, post-abortion syndrome, and healing. Separate chapters allow selection of specialized presentations to accommodate the needs and time constraints of their situations. (List: $34.95; Sale: $24.95.)

Unless otherwise noted on the site itself, shipping is free for all products purchased through www.healthylifepress.com.

Recommended Resources – Books

If God Is So Good, Why Do I Hurt So Bad?, by David B. Biebel, DMin – In this best-selling classic (over 200,000 copies in print worldwide, in five languages) on the subject of loss and renewal, first published in 1989, the author comes alongside people in pain, and shows the way through and beyond it, to joy again. This book has proven helpful to those who are struggling and to those who wish to understand and help. (Printed book: $12.95; PDF eBook: $8.95; both together: $19.95, direct from publisher; eBook reader versions available at www.Amazon.com; www.BN.com; www.eChristian.com.)

52 Ways to Feel Great Today, by David B. Biebel, DMin, James E. Dill, MD, and Bobbie Dill, RN – **Increase Your Vitality, Improve your Outlook.** Simple, fun, inexpensive things you can do to increase your vitality and improve your outlook. Why live an "ordinary" life when you could be experiencing the extraordinary? Don't settle for good enough when "great" is such a short stretch away. Make today great! (Printed book: $14.99.)

VOWS, a Romantic novel by F. F. Whitestone – When the police cruiser pulled up to the curb outside, Faith Framingham's heart skipped a beat, for she could see that Chuck, who should have been driving, was not in the vehicle. Chuck's partner, Sandy, stepped out slowly. Sandy's pursed lips and ashen face spoke volumes. Faith waited by the front door, her hands clasped tightly, to counter the fact that her mind was already reeling. "Love never fails." A compelling story. (Printed book: $12.99; PDF eBook: $9.99; both together, $19.99, direct from publisher; eBook reader versions available at www.Amazon.com; www.BN.com; www.eChristian.com.)

New Light on Depression, a CBA Gold Medallion winner, by David B. Biebel, DMin, and Harold Koenig, MD – The most exhaustive Christian resource on a subject that is more common than we might wish. Hope for those with depression and help for those who love them. (Printed book: $15.00.)

The A to Z Guide To Healthier Living, by David B. Biebel, DMin, James E. Dill, MD, and Bobbie Dill, RN – You'll find great info on: avoiding fad diets, being kind to your GI tract, building healthy bones, finding contentment, getting a good night's sleep, keeping your relationships strong, simplifying your life, staying creative, and much more. (Printed book: 12.99.)

The Secret of Singing Springs, by Monte Swan – One Colorado family's treasure-hunting adventure along the trail of Jesse James. *The Secret of Singing Springs* is written to capture for children and their parents the spirit of the hunt—the hunt for treasure as in God's Truth, which is the objective of walking the Way of Wisdom that is described in the book of Proverbs. (Printed book: $12.99; PDF eBook: $9.99; both together: $19.99, direct from publisher; eBook reader versions at www.Amazon.com; www.BN.com; www.eChristian.com.) **NEWLY RELEASED IN 2013.**

God Loves You Circle, by Michelle Johnson – Daily inspiration for your deeper walk with Christ. This collection of short stories of Christian living will make you laugh, make you cry, but most of all make you contemplate—the meaning and value of walking with the Master moment-by-moment, day-by-day. (**Full-color book: $17.95**; full-color PDF eBook: $9.99; both together: $23.99, direct from the publisher; eBook reader versions available at www.Amazon.com; www.BN.com; www.eChristian.com. **NEWLY RELEASED IN 2013.**

MORE NEW BOOKS FROM HEALTHY LIFE PRESS - 2013

Our God-Given Senses, by Gary A. Burlingame – Did you know humans have NINE senses? The Bible draws on these senses to reveal spiritual truth. We are to taste and see that the Lord is a good. We are to carry the fragrance of Christ. Our faith is produced upon hearing. Jesus asked Thomas to touch him. God created us for a sensory experience and that is what you will find in this book. (Printed book: $12.99; PDF eBook: $9.99; both together: $19.99, direct from publisher; eBook reader versions available at www.Amazon. com; www.BN.com; www.eChristian.com. Available Spring 2013.)

I AM – Transformed in Him – by Diana Burg and Kim Tapfer, a meditative women's Bible study of the I AM statements of Christ in two 6-week volumes or one 12-week volume. Throughout this six week study you will begin to unearth the treasure trove of riches that are found within God's name, I AM WHO I AM. (Printed book: $12.99; PDF eBook: $9.99; both together: $19.99, direct from publisher; eBook reader versions available at www.Amazon.com; www.BN.com; www.eChristian.com.)

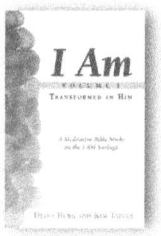

Worth the Cost?, by Jack Tsai, MD – The author was happily on his way to obtaining the American Dream until he decided to take seriously Jesus' command to "Come, follow me." Join him as he explores the cost of medical education and Christian discipleship. Planning to serve God in your future vocation? Take care that your desires do not get side-tracked by the false promises of this world. What you should be doing now so when you are done with your training you will still want to serve God. (Printed book: $12.99, PDF eBook: $9.99; both together: $19.99, direct from publisher; eBook reader versions available: www.Amazon.com; www.BN.com; www.eChristian.com.)

Nature: God's Second Book – An Essential Link to Restoring Your Personal Health and Wellness: Body, Mind, and Spirit, by Elvy P. Rolle – An inspirational book that looks at nature across the chronological and life seasons. It uses the biblical Emmaus Journey as an analogy for life's journey, and offers ideas for using nature appreciation and exploration to reduce life's stresses. The author shares her personal story of how she came to grips with this concept after three trips to the emergency room. (Full-color printed book: $12.99, direct from publisher only; PDF eBook $8.99; both together: $16.99, direct from publisher only; eBook reader versions available at www.Amazon.com; www.BN.com; www.eChristian.com.)

About Healthy Life Press

Healthy Life Press was founded with a primary goal of helping previously unpublished authors to get their works to market, and to reissue worthy, previously published works that were no longer available. Our mission is to help people toward optimal vitality by providing resources promoting physical, emotional, spiritual, and relational health as viewed from a Christian perspective. We see health as a verb, and achieving optimal health as a process—a crucial process for followers of Christ if we are to love the Lord with all our heart, soul, mind, AND strength, and our neighbors as ourselves—for as long as He leaves us here. We are a collaborative and cooperative small Christian publisher. We share costs/we share proceeds.

For information about publishing with us, e-mail: healthylifepress@aol.com.

www.ingramcontent.com/pod-product-compliance
Lightning Source LLC
Chambersburg PA
CBHW070640050426
42451CB00008B/244

What People are Saying

Beautifully written and inspiring words always—thank you!!
– Michelle K.

You are an awesome woman of God, put here for a very special reason. I look forward to reading your very inspiring posts daily. Keep on shining for God.
– Sharon D.

Your words are very touching and inspiring. I don't know your life or know your struggles, but you are an amazing woman of God. I thank you for posting your inspiring messages. Continue to bless us, because you never know whose heart you're speaking to.
– Staci H.

Your words lift me up and encourage me to be the woman God sees in me.
– Alex N.

You have a glow, from your words of faith, to draw in those that need to hear the Word and the actual stories from the Bible, to understanding. Thank you. And God bless you.
– Laura H.

You have spoken to me and touched my heart with your writings. God bless you and yours always!
– Rayna A.